# Big Splash Knits

## MITTENS, HATS, SOCKS, AND MORE
## FROM ATLANTIC CANADA

**SHIRLEY A. SCOTT**

BOULDER
BOOKS

Library and Archives Canada Cataloguing in Publication

Title: Big splash knits : mittens, hats, socks, and more from Atlantic Canada / Shirley A. Scott.

Names: Scott, Shirley A., author

Description: Series statement: Saltwater knits

Identifiers: Canadiana 20240425979 | ISBN 9781998220168 (softcover)

Subjects: LCSH: Knitting—Atlantic Provinces—Patterns. | LCSH: Knitwear—Atlantic Provinces. | LCSH: Knitting—Atlantic Provinces.

Classification: LCC TT819.C32 A85 2024 | DDC 746.43/20432—dc23

© 2024 Shirley A. Scott

Design and layout: Todd Manning

Cover photo: Anja Sajovic Photography

Editor: Stephanie Porter

Copy editor: Iona Bulgin

Printed in China

Published by Boulder Books

Portugal Cove-St. Philip's, Newfoundland and Labrador

www.boulderbooks.ca

We acknowledge the financial support of the Government of Newfoundland and Labrador through the Department of Tourism, Culture, Industry and Innovation.

Funded by the Government of Canada    Financé par le gouvernement du Canada    Canada

For Katherine

Whose ocean devotion
was deep and wide

# CONTENTS

# FOREWORD

My daughter gave me a pendant with the following words inscribed on it: "In the rhythm of the needles, there is music for the soul." I can think of no better conductor of that rhythm than Shirley Anne Scott.

Shirley has been designing knitting patterns for years. She and co-author Christine LeGrow carefully resurrected dozens of traditional patterns for trigger mitts, socks, vamps, and more in their *Saltwater* series. These books are addictive. My personal copies are dog-eared, splattered with coffee and cat paw prints, well used and well loved. Shirley and Christine have a large social media following that shares their love of knitting, and of Newfoundland and Labrador.

After completing the fourth and final book of that series together, Shirley still had more to share—new designs that spring from her creative knitter's eye and that draw inspiration from the past and present. Thus was born *Big Splash Knits*.

In this book, Shirley offers us what she loves. She fosters the love of knitting among new knitters and among those who have been knitting for longer than some new knitters have been alive. What compels us to sit down with a cup of tea and treasure every page? While looking at photo after photo of gorgeous projects, we gaze at our own yarn, thinking of colours we might use for the perfect gift or perhaps to match our windbreaker. We breathe deeply at the thought of a fresh cast on and smile at the possibilities that lie ahead.

Knitting is creation. Knitting is heritage. Knitting is culture. Knitting is peace. Knitting is love. Leaf through these pages, choose your absolute favourite pattern, get your needles ready, place your chosen yarn side by side until your vision rings clear. And begin.

May Shirley's beautiful rhythmic music fill your soul.

Julie Vogt
Executive Director (and free-time knitter / stash enhancer)
Newfoundland & Labrador Folk Arts Society

# WELCOME

The spirit of place has guided the creation of *Big Splash Knits* every step of the way. We love where we live and we love to knit. What could be better than combining the two and sharing our passions with you? We are not simply knitting the days away here on the edge of the continent. We are taking our place in the great stream of art that graces human lives. What we do is important.

*Big Splash Knits* offers many small, sweet projects, all of which showcase our lives here beside the chilly North Atlantic. We favour the beautiful wool produced by Briggs and Little in York Mills, New Brunswick, in our samples.

It's the "go to" yarn in our part of the world and we are forever thankful for it. Briggs and Little is one of the few remaining woollen mills in Canada. It has been successfully producing a sustainable local product for more than 100 years. Available in many weights and exciting colours, this yarn is strong, affordable, widely sold, and utterly inspiring. If you substitute yarns, choose something in the same yarn weight group and be sure to match the gauge.

Techniques used in *Big Splash Knits* are in general use in the knitting world.

Want to be a neater knitter? Any special technical hijinks are fully described and we offer tips specific to many designs. The book also introduces "Big Splash Knitters Trivia" as a friendly way of explaining "what's been did and what's been hid" in our design process. It's a feast of learning you'll enjoy discussing with others for a long time to come. Perhaps it will address some questions you've had for years. Experience has taught us that technical information is much easier to absorb when it comes in small, specific spoonfuls.

Moments of perfect stillness, intense awareness, and acute anxiety—knitting brings them all. Remember that making mistakes puts a knitter on the path of true learning. We hope this book helps you master greater skills with each new project. Every pattern is assigned a level of difficulty. Gale Force designs are for the courageous. Batten the hatches! They require considerable attention and experience, but we've made sure to include Smooth Sailing patterns to encourage beginners, for relaxed group knitting, for sitting on the beach, or for other forms of *le tricot en plein air*.

It is our great pleasure to celebrate the knitting life on this blue and green planet we call home. We wish you many great moments of the exquisite peace that accompanies good knitting.

Shirley Anne Scott
St. John's, Newfoundland

# HOW TO GRAFT IN KITCHENER STITCH

This method is used at the top of a mitten, on the toe of a sock, and in many other places.

Arrange stitches on two double pointed needles, the same number on each needle. Hold the needles parallel to one another, with the right side of the work facing. Thread the long tail emerging from the back knitting needle into a tapestry needle for sewing.

**Step 1. Front Needle.** Insert the tapestry needle into the first stitch on the knitting needle nearest you (the front needle) as if to knit. Slip this stitch off the needle and pull the yarn gently to imitate the appearance of a knitted stitch.

**Step 2. Front Needle.** Insert the sewing needle into the next stitch on the front needle as if to purl. Tension the yarn gently but leave this stitch on the knitting needle.

**Step 3. Back Needle.** Taking the yarn under the front needle, insert the sewing needle into the first stitch of the back needle as if to purl. Tension the yarn and slip this stitch off the back needle.

**Step 4. Back Needle.** Insert the sewing needle in the next stitch as if to knit. Tension the yarn and leave this stitch on the needle.

Repeat steps 1–4 until 2 stitches remain unworked, one on each knitting needle, ending with step 4. Remove both knitting needles. Darn end of sewing yarn.

## THUMB GUSSETS IN WORDS

● Knit 1 with Dark (D)

Empty square =
Knit 1 with Light (L)

➡ Make 1 Right-leaning stitch with D

⬅ Make 1 Left-leaning stitch with D

⇨ Make 1 Right-leaning stitch with L

⇦ Make 1 Left-leaning stitch with L

### Gusset A (Dark Outline)

Chart rows numbered 1–18 (bottom to top).

## Gusset A in Words
### Size Medium, Large

**Round 1.** Make 1 right-leaning stitch with D, K1D, make 1 left-leaning stitch with D.

**Round 2.** K1D, K1L, K1D.

**Round 3.** K1D, make 1 right with L, K1D, make 1 left with L, K1D.

**Round 4.** K2D, K1L, K2D.

**Round 5.** K1D, make 1 right with D, K1L, K1D, K1L, make 1 left with D, K1D.

**Round 6.** (K1D, K1L) three times, K1D.

**Round 7.** K1D, make 1 right with L, (K1D, K1L) two times, K1D, make 1 left with L, K1D.

**Round 8.** K1D, (K1D, K1L) three times, K2D.

**Round 9.** K1D, make 1 right with D, (K1L, K1D) three times, K1L, make 1 left with D, K1D.

**Round 10.** (K1D, K1L) five times, K1D.

**Round 11.** K1D, make 1 right with L, (K1D, K1L) four times, K1D, make 1 left with L, K1D.

**Round 12.** K1D, (K1D, K1L) five times, K2D.

**Round 13.** K1D, make 1 right with D, (K1L, K1D) five times, K1L, make 1 left with D, K1D.

**Round 14.** (K1D, K1L) seven times, K1D (15 stitches).

**Size Large Only. Round 15.** K1D, make 1 right with L, (K1D, K1L) six times, K1D, make 1 left with L, K1D.

**Round 16.** K1D, (K1D, K1L) seven times, K2D.

**Round 17.** K1D, make 1 right with D, (K1L, K1D) seven times, K1L, make 1 left with D, K1D.

**Round 18.** (K1D, K1L) nine times, K1D (19 stitches).

## Gusset B (Light Outline)

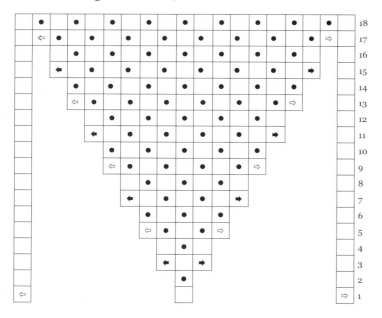

## Gusset B in Words
### Size Medium, Large

**Round 1.** Make 1 right-leaning stitch with L, K1L, make 1 left-leaning stitch with L.

**Round 2.** K1L, K1D, K1L.

**Round 3.** K1L, make 1 right with D, K1L, make 1 left with D, K1L.
**Round 4.** K2L, K1D, K2L.

**Round 5.** K1L, make 1 right with L, K1D, K1L, K1D, make 1 left with L, K1L.

**Round 6.** (K1L, K1D) three times, K1L.

**Round 7.** K1L, make 1 right with D, (K1L, K1D) two times, K1L, make 1 left with D, K1L.

**Round 8.** K1L, (K1L, K1D) three times, K2L.

**Round 9.** K1L, make 1 right with L, (K1D, K1L) three times, K1D, make 1 left with L, K1L.

**Round 10.** (K1L, K1D) five times, K1L.

**Round 11.** K1L, make 1 right with D, (K1L, K1D) four times, K1L, make 1 left with D, K1L.

**Round 12.** K1L, (K1L, K1D) five times, K2L.

**Round 13.** K1L, make 1 right with L, (K1D, K1L) five times, K1D, make 1 left with L, K1L.

**Round 14.** (K1L, K1D) seven times, K1L (15 stitches).

**Size Large Only. Round 15.** K1L, make 1 right with D, (K1L, K1D) six times, K1L, make 1 left with D, K1L.

**Round 16.** K2L, (K1D, K1L) seven times, K1L.

**Round 17.** K1L, make 1 right with L, (K1D, K1L) seven times, K1D, make 1 left with L, K1L.

**Round 18.** (K1L, K1D) nine times, K1L (19 stitches).

# TREETOPS
## Wristers, Classic Mittens, and Trigger Mitts

**DEGREE OF DIFFICULTY** \* \* \* **Gale Force**

We are privileged to live where trees are abundant, soaking up carbon emissions and breathing out their lifegiving oxygen. A horizon of dark green forested hills is a tonic for the spirit. In our region, trees may be tall and stately or bent and gnarled from exposure to strong winds. These tough little trees are sometimes called tuckamore. They are dear to our hearts.

This simple triangle pattern is very old and is known in many countries. It's a breeze to knit in different styles and sizes. Changing contrast colours every third or sixth round means lots of fun for the imaginative knitter.

### SIZE

**Large.** Circumference: 10 inches (25.5 cm). Length from beginning of Treetops pattern: 7.5 inches (19 cm), or as desired.

**Medium.** Circumference: 8 inches (21 cm). Length from beginning of Treetops pattern: 7 inches (18 cm), or as desired.

### YOU NEED

Two or more shades of light worsted weight yarn (Group 3). 250 metres of Dark (D) and 250 metres of Light (L) are usually

enough to make a pair of trigger mitts plus a pair of wristers. Oddments of L are sufficient for multicoloured mitts. Samples were knit with Briggs and Little Regal 100% wool.

One set of 4.00 mm double pointed needles. Two thinner double pointed needles (optional) are useful for Three-Needle Bind Off only. Ring markers.

## GAUGE

24 stitches and 28 rows = 4 inches (10 cm).

**TREETOPS Chart**

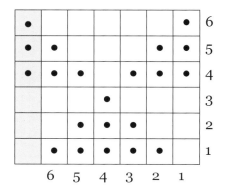

# THUMB GUSSET Chart

Or follow Gusset B in the Gussets in Words section

## CHART SYMBOLS

- • K1D

  Empty square = K1L

- ← Make 1 Left with D

  → Make 1 Right with D

- ⇦ Make 1 Left with L

  ⇨ Make 1 Right with L

## SALT AND PEPPER PATTERN (S&P)

**Round 1.** (K1D, K1L).
**Round 2.** (K1L, K1D).

Work charts from right to left, bottom to top. Always carry D on the left and L on the right to prevent streaks in work.

Size Large is presented first, followed by Medium in parentheses. If only one number is given, it applies to both sizes.

Instructions apply to both hands unless otherwise indicated.

## CAST ON

Cast on 42 (36) stitches for the wrist. Divide evenly on 3 needles and join in a circle, being careful not to twist. Work 30 (24–27) rounds of (K2, P1) ribbing, or desired length, in a striped pattern of your choice.

**Increase Round.** Knit 1 round, increasing 17 (13) stitches evenly spaced, 59 (49) stitches. Arrange work on needles: 31, 14, 14 (25, 12, 12) stitches.

Note that on some thumb gusset rounds there will be 2 or more adjacent stitches of the same colour. This is corrected on the following round. Use Gusset B in the Gussets in Words instead of the Thumb Gusset chart, if preferred.

**Set-Up. Round 1. Right Hand.** Join new colour, and keeping D on the left (ahead) throughout, work stitches 1–6 of Round 1 Treetops chart 5 (4) times. Work last highlighted stitch of chart. These 31 (25) stitches form the front of the mitten. **Palm.** K1D, K1L, K1D, place marker. Make 1 right-leaning stitch with L, K1L. Make 1 left-leaning stitch with L, place marker. (K1D, K1L) to end of round.

**Set-Up. Round 1. Left Hand.** Join new colour and, keeping D on the left (ahead) throughout, work Round 1 of Treetops chart for 31 (25) stitches for front, as for Right Hand. **Palm.** (K1D, K1L) until 4 stitches remain in round, K1D, place marker. Make 1 right-leaning stitch with L, K1L. Make 1 left-leaning stitch with L. Place marker. K1D, K1L.

**Both Hands.** This sets up Treetops on the front, S&P on the palm, and Round 1 of the thumb gusset between the markers.

**Set-Up. Round 2.** Work Treetops Round 2 on front. **Palm.** Work in S&P to marker, slip marker. Work Round 2 of Thumb Gusset chart (or use Gusset B in Thumb Gussets in Words) to next marker, slip marker. Work S&P to end of round.

Continue working successive rounds of patterns as established until thumb gusset is complete (Large: Round 18) (Medium: Round 14), finishing the round in S&P. There will be 19 (15) gusset stitches between markers.

**Next Round.** Work next round of Treetops on front. **Palm.** Work S&P to marker, remove marker. Place gusset stitches on a piece of waste yarn, remove marker. Cast on 1 stitch with L to bridge gap. Work S&P to end of round, 59 (49) stitches. Thumb gusset is complete.

Continue working Treetops on the front and S&P on the palm until 30 (24) Treetops rounds are complete, finishing the round in S&P.

Proceed to Classic Mittens or Trigger Mitts if desired.

## WRISTERS

**Top Trim.** With the trim colour of your choice, knit 1 round.

**Next Round. Large.** (K2, P1, K2, P2tog) until 3 stitches remain, K2, P1 (51 stitches). **Medium.** (K2, P1, K2, P2tog) to end of round (42 stitches). **Next Round.** Work (K2, P1) rib to end of round. Cast off in ribbing.

### TIPS

When working wrist ribbing, join new colours on the last purl stitch of the previous round instead of the first knit stitch of the new round. This minimizes the jog where colours meet.

Wristers fit best when the ribbed cuff is extra long.

**Thumb Trim.** Transfer gusset stitches to 2 double pointed needles. Join the colour of your choice and knit these stitches. Pick up and knit 2 (3) stitches at the base of the thumb (21 stitches, 18 stitches). Arrange work on 3 needles and work 2 rounds of (K2, P1) rib. Cast off in rib.

## CLASSIC MITTENS

Work Treetops Rounds 1–6 on front and S&P on palm.

**Next Round.** Beginning with K1L, work in S&P to end of round.

**Large Only.** Work 1 round more of S&P, or continue until work measures 2 inches (5 cm) from tip of mitten.

**Medium Only.** Work 8 rounds more in S&P, or until work reaches tip of little finger.

**Both Hands. Shape Top.** Use Two-Step Shaping, as follows.

**Shaping Round 1. Front.** With Treetops facing, K1 in correct colour. SSK with the next colour in the sequence. Resume S&P on the next stitch (having made 2 adjacent stitches of the same colour). Work in S&P until 3 stitches remain on front. K2tog in the same colour as the stitch just made. Work last stitch in correct colour of sequence. **Palm.** As front.

**Shaping Round 2. Front.** K1, SSK in next colour in the sequence. S&P until 3 stitches remain on front. K2tog in next colour in the sequence, K1. **Palm.** As front. Correct colour sequence is restored.

Repeat these 2 shaping rounds until 11 (9) stitches remain. Break yarns. Thread one into a yarn needle and pass through remaining stitches knitwise. Pull tight and fasten. Proceed to Thumb.

## TRIGGER MITTS

**Large Only.** Rearrange stitches on needles: 30, 15, 14.

**Next Round.** Beginning with K1L, work in S&P to end of round.

**Left Hand Only.** Break yarns.

**Reserve Trigger Finger Stitches.** With Treetops facing, at the same edge of the mitten as the thumb, place 8 stitches from the front and corresponding 8 stitches from the palm on holders for the trigger finger.

**Next Round. Right Hand.** With Treetops facing, work in S&P to the gap. Cast on 2 stitches in pattern to bridge gap. Work in S&P to end of round: 45 (35) stitches.

Back from a good weekend at Rodmell ... with the Maytree like a breaking wave outside; all the garden green tunnels, mounds of green.

Virginia Woolf, from her diaries

**Next Round. Left Hand.** With Treetops facing, rejoin yarns at the first stitch on the front after the trigger finger. This is the new beginning of the round. Work S&P on the front and palm to the gap. Cast on 2 stitches in pattern to bridge gap: 45 (35) stitches.

**Next Round. Both Hands.** Work in S&P to end of round. Arrange stitches: 22, 12, 11 (17, 9, 9). Knit 12 (14) rounds more in S&P, or until work reaches the tip of the little finger.

**Shape Top.** Note that some rounds will produce adjacent stitches of the same colour. Use Three-Step Shaping for a rounded top as follows.

**Shaping Round 1. Front.** With Treetops facing, K1 in correct colour. SSK with the next colour in the sequence. Resume S&P on the next stitch (having made 2 adjacent stitches of the same colour). Work in pattern until 3 stitches remain on front. K2tog in the same colour as the stitch just made. Work last stitch in correct colour. **Palm.** As front.

**Shaping Round 2. Front.** K1, SSK in next colour in the sequence. S&P until 3 stitches remain on front. K2tog in next colour in the sequence, K1. **Palm.** As front. Correct colour sequence is restored.

**Round 3.** Work in S&P without decreasing.

Repeat this three-round sequence twice more: 21 (19) stitches. Break yarns, leaving a 16-inch tail with one colour.

**Three-Needle Bind Off.** The hand is finished with a Three-Needle Bind Off on the wrong side of the work.

Place stitches of front on a length of waste yarn. Place stitches of palm on another length of yarn. Turn mitten inside out to work bind off on the wrong side using the long tail.

Return stitches on holders to 2 thinner double pointed needles for easier working. Hold these needles parallel to one another, the needle with the larger number of stitches nearest you. With a third double pointed needle and the long tail, K1 from the front holding needle. Then knit 1 stitch from this needle together with 1 stitch of the opposite colour from the rear needle: 2 stitches now on the working needle. Pass first stitch on working needle over second stitch to cast it off. 1 stitch remains on working needle. Continue to knit together 1 stitch from front and rear holding needles and slipping the first stitch over the second stitch on the working needle to cast off. Repeat until 1 stitch remains on working needle. Fasten off and darn ends. Turn work right side out.

## THUMB

Transfer thumb stitches from holder to 2 double pointed needles. Rejoin yarns and knit these stitches in S&P. With another needle, pick up and knit 2 (4) stitches in S&P at the base of the thumb: 21 (19) stitches. Note beginning of round. Work 15 (12) rounds more in S&P, or until work reaches the tip of the thumb. Work Finger Decrease Rounds 1–2.

**Finger Decrease Round 1.** (K1 with correct colour in the S&P sequence, SSK with next colour in the sequence, K1 in S&P), repeat to end of round, working any leftover stitches in S&P. Adjacent stitches in the same colour will be eliminated in the next round.

**Finger Decrease Round 2.** (K1 with correct S&P colour, SSK with next colour in the S&P sequence) to end of round, working any leftover stitches in S&P. Break yarns. Thread through remaining stitches knitwise and secure.

## TRIGGER FINGER

Transfer stitches from front holder to a double pointed needle. Place stitches from palm on a double pointed needle.

**Right Trigger Finger.** With Treetops facing, rejoin yarns and work in S&P to the gap. Pick up and knit 5 (3) stitches in correct S&P sequence from the base of the hand: 21 (19) stitches.

**Left Trigger Finger.** With Treetops facing, rejoin yarns, working stitches of front in S&P. Pick up and knit 5 (3) stitches in S&P from the base of the hand. Work palm stitches in S&P, 21 (19) stitches.

**Both Hands.** Note beginning of round. Divide stitches conveniently on 3 double pointed needles and work 16 (14) rounds more of S&P, or until work reaches the tip of the index finger. Work Finger Decrease Rounds 1–2 as for Thumb.

**FINISHING.** Darn ends securely. Press lightly, omitting ribbing.

© Shirley A. Scott 2024

# NIGHT SKY
## Classic Mittens for the Midnight Hour

**DEGREE OF DIFFICULTY** * * **Choppy**

In our part of the world, we are blessed with thrilling night skies. They shine with ethereal beauty on the glacial nights of deepest winter. In the sweet darkness of late summer, gathered around our campfires, we eagerly await the Perseid meteor showers.

It's easy to understand the power attributed to stars. They shaped mythologies in many early civilizations. The Maya used star maps to site some of their jungle cities. At our northern latitudes, we know them best as navigational aids and joy-bringers.

Pictorial patterns such as Night Sky are fun to knit. The picture develops quickly, row by row. This pattern also features large areas of a single shade where the unused colour must be carried loosely on the inside and woven in frequently.

I dream of a winter with long, dark nights and thick snow on the ground. I want to wrap the kids up and build snowmen with them. Instead, we're scrabbling around in little white patches on the lawn, trying to find enough powder for a snowball.

Steve Backshall, journalist

The instructions include two unusual brain-teasers. First, carry the Light yarn on the left instead of the right. This ensures a very sharp image. Second, to increase the clarity of the chart, an empty square represents a Dark stitch and a dot represents a Light stitch, the reverse of most designs. After a round or two, this becomes easy.

## SIZE

**Medium.** Circumference: 8 inches (21 cm). Length from beginning of Night Sky pattern to tip: 7 inches (18 cm), or as desired. For custom sizes, change gauge.

## YOU NEED

Two shades of light worsted weight yarn (Group 3). 125 metres of Dark (D) and 125 metres of Light (L). Samples were knit with Briggs and Little Regal 100% wool.

One set of 4.00 mm double pointed needles. Two thinner double pointed needles (optional) are useful for Three-Needle Bind Off only. Ring markers.

## GAUGE

24 stitches and 28 rows = 4 inches (10 cm).

Come, shape your plans where the fire is bright,
And the shimmering glasses are,
When the woods are white in the winter's night,
Under the northern star.

Albert Bigelow Paine,
*The Tent Dwellers*

# NIGHT SKY Right Hand

# NIGHT SKY Left Hand

## THUMB GUSSET Chart

| | | | | | | | | | | | | | | | | Row |
|---|---|---|---|---|---|---|---|---|---|---|---|---|---|---|---|---|
| | • | | • | | • | | • | | • | | • | | • | | | 14 |
| ⇦ | • | | • | | • | | • | | • | | • | | ⇨ | | | 13 |
| | | • | | • | | • | | • | | • | | | | | | 12 |
| | | ← | | • | | • | | • | | • | | → | | | | 11 |
| | | | • | | • | | • | | • | | • | | | | | 10 |
| | ⇦ | • | | • | | • | | • | | • | ⇨ | | | | | 9 |
| | | | | • | | • | | • | | | | | | | | 8 |
| | | | ← | | • | | • | | • | | → | | | | | 7 |
| | | | | • | | • | | • | | | | | | | | 6 |
| | | | ⇦ | • | | • | | ⇨ | | | | | | | | 5 |
| | | | | | • | | | | | | | | | | | 4 |
| | | | | ← | | → | | | | | | | | | | 3 |
| | | | | | • | | | | | | | | | | | 2 |
| ⇦ | | | | | | | | | | | | | | | ⇨ | 1 |

## CHART SYMBOLS

- • K1L                                  Empty square = K1D

➡ Make 1 Right with L          ⬅ Make 1 Left with L

⇨ Make 1 Right with D          ⇦ Make 1 Left with D

Digits in red = the number of D stitches
before the next L stitch

## BIG SPLASH TRIVIA

**Why Carry Dark on the Left or Right?**

Why do we usually carry Dark on the left (ahead) and Light on the right in Fair Isle knitting? Perhaps it would be more accurate to speak in terms of background colour on the left and stitch pattern colour on the right.

Because we are not robots, the yarn carried on the left makes a stitch of a slightly different appearance than the yarn carried on the right. The difference is clearly visible on the wrong side of the work but not always obvious on the right. In geometric patterns such as the diamonds, squares, and triangles of many mitten designs, the difference is not very noticeable, but if you change back and forth, carrying Dark sometimes on the left and sometimes on the right, the result is messy. And in pictorial designs such as this one, it is disastrous.

In our opinion, carrying the Light shade on the left in Night Sky makes the picture much sharper and clearer. Nevertheless, it's a matter of choice. Experiment! Feel free to use any colour in any position, but use it consistently.

## NIGHT SKY Thumb Gusset in Words

**Round 1.** Make 1 right-leaning stitch with D, K1D, make 1 left-leaning stitch with D.

**Round 2.** K1D, K1L, K1D.

**Round 3.** K1D, make 1 right with L, K1D, make 1 left with L, K1D.

**Round 4.** K2D, K1L, K2D.

**Round 5.** K1D, make 1 right with D, K1L, K1D, K1L, make 1 left with D, K1D.

**Round 6.** (K1D, K1L) three times, K1D.

**Round 7.** K1D, make 1 right with L, (K1D, K1L) twice, K1D, make 1 left with L, K1D.

**Round 8.** K1D, (K1D, K1L) three times, K2D.

**Round 9.** K1D, make 1 right with D, (K1L, K1D) three times, K1L, make 1 left with D, K1D.

**Round 10.** (K1D, K1L) five times, K1D.

**Round 11.** K1D, make 1 right with L, (K1D, K1L) four times, K1D, make 1 left with L, K1D.

**Round 12.** K1D, (K1D, K1L) five times, K2D.

**Round 13.** K1D, make 1 right with D, (K1L, K1D) five times, K1L, make 1 left with D, K1D.

**Round 14.** (K1D, K1L) seven times, K1D.

### SALT AND PEPPER PATTERN (S&P)
**Round 1.** (K1D, K1L).
**Round 2.** (K1L, K1D).

Work charts from right to left, bottom to top.

**For best results, carry L on the left (ahead) and D on the right.**

**Note that chart symbols are different from other patterns.Remember that a blank square represents a D stitch, not an L stitch.**

If preferred, use Night Sky Thumb Gusset in Words for the stitches between the markers. Note that on some thumb gusset rounds there will be two or more adjacent stitches of the same colour. This is corrected on the following round.

Instructions are for both hands unless otherwise indicated.

### CAST ON
With D, cast on 36 stitches. Divide evenly on 3 needles and join in a circle, being careful not to twist. Work 27–30 rounds of (K2, P1) ribbing in a solid or striped pattern of your choice.

**Increase Round.** With D, knit 1 round, increasing 13 stitches evenly spaced (49 stitches). Arrange work on needles: 25, 12, 12 stitches.

**Set-Up. Round 1. Right Hand.** Join L and work Round 1 of Night Sky Right Hand on 25 stitches for front of mitten. **Palm.** K1D, K1L, place marker. Make 1 right-leaning stitch with D, K1D, make 1 left-leaning stitch with D, place marker. Work (K1L, K1D) to last stitch, K1L.

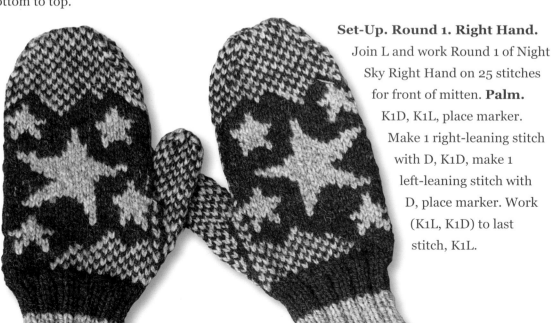

**Set-Up. Round 1. Left Hand.** Join L and work Round 1 of Night Sky Left Hand for 25 stitches for front. **Palm.** (K1D, K1L) until 2 stitches remain in round, place marker. M1R with D, K1D, M1L with D, place marker. K1L.

**Both Hands.** This sets up 25 Night Sky stitches on the front, 24 S&P stitches on the palm, and Round 1 of the thumb gusset between the markers.

**Set-Up. Round 2.** Work Round 2 of the correct Night Sky chart on front. **Palm.** Work in S&P to marker, slip marker. Work Round 2 of thumb gusset to next marker, slip marker. Work S&P to end of round.

Continue in pattern as established until thumb gusset Round 14 is complete, finishing the round in S&P. There will be 15 gusset stitches between markers.

**Next Round.** Work next round of Night Sky pattern on front. **Palm.** Work S&P to marker, remove marker. Place gusset stitches on a length of waste yarn, remove marker. Cast on 1 stitch with correct colour to bridge gap. Work S&P to end of round (49 stitches). Thumb gusset is complete.

Continue working Night Sky on the front and S&P on the palm until 39 Night Sky rounds are complete, finishing the round in S&P.

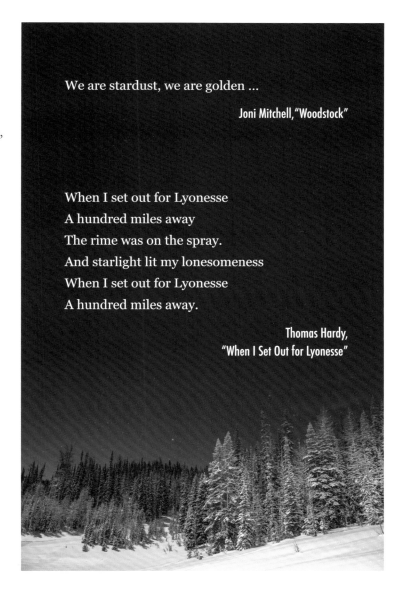

We are stardust, we are golden ...

Joni Mitchell, "Woodstock"

When I set out for Lyonesse
A hundred miles away
The rime was on the spray.
And starlight lit my lonesomeness
When I set out for Lyonesse
A hundred miles away.

Thomas Hardy,
"When I Set Out for Lyonesse"

**Next Round.** Arrange stitches: 24, 12, 13. Work one round more in S&P, or continue in S&P until work reaches the tip of the little finger.

**Shape Top.** Use Three-Step Shaping for a rounded top, as follows. Note that some rounds will produce adjacent stitches of the same colour. This is corrected on the following round.

**Shaping Round 1. Front.** With Night Sky facing, K1 in correct S&P colour. SSK with the next colour in the sequence. Resume S&P on the next stitch. Work in S&P until 3 stitches remain on front. K2tog in the same colour as the stitch just made. Work last stitch in correct colour. **Palm.** As front.

**Shaping Round 2. Front.** K1, SSK in next colour in the sequence. Work in S&P until 3 stitches remain on front. K2tog in next colour in the sequence, K1. **Palm.** As front. Correct colour sequence is restored.

**Shaping Round 3.** Work in S&P without decreasing. Repeat this three-round sequence twice more (25 stitches). Break yarns, leaving a 16-inch tail with one colour.

**Three-Needle Bind Off.** The hand is finished with a Three-Needle Bind Off on the wrong side of the work.

Place stitches of front on a length of waste yarn. Place stitches of palm on another length of yarn. Turn mitten inside out to work bind off on the wrong side using the long tail. Return stitches on holders to 2 thinner double pointed needles for easier working. Hold these needles parallel to one another, the needle with the larger number of stitches nearest you. With a third double pointed needle and the long tail, K1 from the front holding needle. Then knit 1 stitch from this needle together with 1 stitch of the opposite colour from the rear needle: 2 stitches now on the working needle. Pass first stitch on working needle over second stitch to cast it off. 1 stitch remains on working needle. Continue to knit together 1 stitch from front and rear holding needles and slipping the first stitch over second stitch on the working needle to cast off. Repeat until 1 stitch remains on working needle. Fasten off and darn ends. Turn work right side out. Do not poke out the corners.

## THUMB

Transfer thumb stitches from holder to 2 double pointed needles. Rejoin yarns and knit these stitches in S&P. With another needle, pick up and knit 4 stitches in S&P at the base of the thumb (19 stitches). Note beginning of round. Work 12 rounds more in S&P, or until work reaches the tip of the thumb. Work Thumb Decrease Rounds 1–2.

**Thumb Decrease Round 1.** (K1 with correct colour in the S&P sequence, SSK with next colour in the sequence, K1 in S&P), repeat to end of round, working any leftover stitches in S&P. Adjacent stitches in the same colour will be eliminated in the next round.

**Thumb Decrease Round 2.** (K1 with correct S&P colour, SSK with next colour in the S&P sequence) to end of round, working any leftover stitches in S&P. Break yarns. Thread through remaining stitches knitwise and secure.

**FINISHING.** Darn ends securely. Press lightly, omitting ribbing.

© Shirley A. Scott 2024

## TIPS

Pay close attention to the chart symbols! In this design, a blank square indicates a Dark stitch, not a Light one.

When possible, avoid weaving in a yarn directly above a weave in the previous round. Look for a free stitch in the round below, then weave in above it.

# NECK LACE
## Dress-Up Scarf

**DEGREE OF DIFFICULTY** ✶✶ **Choppy**

Lace, a work of art made of air and thread, has been likened to a frill on the ocean. Some of the world's best lace knitters live in exposed places such as the remote Shetland archipelago, surrounded by water and blown by winds. We are always amazed by the great beauty created in rugged places.

Knit flat in a single colour, Neck Lace gives knitters a break from the anxiety of choosing and working with colours. Our sample was made with sport weight yarn, but other weights work just as well when paired with suitable needles. Make your lace short, chic, and narrow or wide and enveloping by simply adding or subtracting a few stitches at cast on. The long and winding road of scarf knitting brings great pleasure, but it takes time, motivation, and concentration. It can't be rushed. We have shortened ours and seamed it to make an easy-to-wear circle. You may prefer a traditional long scarf.

Why does the wrong side of neckwear always seem to work its way front and centre when worn in public? That will never happen with our Neck Lace. A clever combination of yarn overs and slipped stitches makes it totally reversible. It's also sturdy, not delicate.

Live a little! Cut a dashing figure wearing your lace with a leather jacket or kid gloves. Wear a few twinkling jewels. Or maybe a pair of high leather boots and a touch of rich velvet.

He'd a French cocked-hat on his forehead,
    a bunch of lace at his chin,
A coat of the claret velvet, and breeches
    of brown doeskin.
They fitted with never a wrinkle.
    His boots were up to the thigh.
And he rode with a jeweled twinkle
His pistol butts a-twinkle,
His rapier hilt a-twinkle, under the jeweled sky.

**Alfred Noyes, "The Highwayman"**

## SIZE

Length: 25 inches (63.5 cm), or as desired. Width: 5 inches (12.5 cm), or as desired. Change the width by adding or subtracting cast-on stitches in groups of 5.

## YOU NEED

Approximately 250 yards (225 m) of sport or fingering weight yarn (Group 2) for a very generous length, or as desired. Sample was knit with Briggs and Little Sport.

Two 4.00 mm needles.

## TIPS

Even though it will be worn next to the skin, a firm wool yarn is better than an ultrasoft silk or merino yarn for this project. It adds body.

It is easy to lose your place in these instructions. Rows 1 and 3 are simpler rows with no yarnovers. Mark this side of the work with a safety pin marker, as a reminder to breathe. The slipped stitches at the end of each row wrap around to make an excellent firm selvage, but they also make it difficult to unravel mistakes. Consider trying the pattern with waste yarn before beginning.

Experienced lace knitters will expect to work K2tog after a yarnover. Don't do it!

**Why Slip Stitches Knitwise or Purlwise?**

In general, if stitches are simply being moved from one place (or one needle) to another, slip them purlwise. Slipping them knitwise in this case would twist the stitches. Transfer stitches from waste yarn to needles purlwise also.

If stitches are actually part of a pattern or stitch sequence such as SKP (slip, knit, pass), they should be slipped knitwise. Always slip knitwise to close the tip of a picket-fence mitten or a thumb. Slip all stitches knitwise in our Neck Lace design.

## GAUGE

Gauge is not critical in this design.

Psso = pass slipped stitch over.
Slip all stitches as if to knit.

## CAST ON

Cast on 40 stitches, or any multiple of 5 stitches, to reach desired width.

**Row 1.** (K3, P2) to last 5 stitches. K3, P1. Leaving yarn in front, slip the last stitch.

**Row 2.** (K1, yarn over, K1, with yarn in back slip 1 knitwise, P2, with yarn in back psso) to last 3 stitches. Slip 1, P1. With yarn in front slip 1, psso.

**Row 3.** (K2, P3) to last 5 stitches. K2, P2. With yarn in front, slip last stitch.

**Row 4.** (Slip 1, K2, psso, P1, yarn over purlwise, P1, yarn to back) to last 2 stitches. P1, yarn over purlwise, with yarn in front, slip the last stitch knitwise.

Repeat these four rows until work reaches desired length, finishing with Row 1 or Row 3. Cast off gently in pattern.

## FINISHING

Set the stitches firmly by pressing this scarf on both front and back with steam or a damp cloth. Seam the ends gently, creating a circle if desired. **Optional.** Wrap a length of yarn around the scarf, gather it in a little and tie it around the width of the scarf. This creates a stylish shape but can be easily removed if desired.

# SEESAW SEA
## Nautical Mitts

### DEGREE OF DIFFICULTY ** Choppy

We never tire of wave patterns. These bold billows are inspired by the cobblestones seen in some Iberian cities. They remind us of early Basque endeavours in our part of the world. When the young Samuel de Champlain first sailed the northwest Atlantic on a voyage of exploration, he was astonished to come upon Basques, who had been quietly fishing these waters for 40 seasons.

### SIZE

**Medium.** Circumference: 8 inches (21 cm). Length from beginning of Seesaw Sea pattern to tip: 6.5 inches (18.5 cm), or as desired.

### YOU NEED

Two or more shades of light worsted weight yarn (Group 3): 125 metres of Dark (D) and 125 metres of Light (L). Samples were knit with Briggs and Little Regal 100% wool.

One set of 4.00 mm double pointed needles. Ring markers.

### GAUGE

24 stitches and 28 rows = 4 inches (10 cm).

The only sea I saw was the seesaw sea ...

Dylan Thomas, *Under Milk Wood*

## SEESAW SEA Chart

| | | | | | | | | |
|---|---|---|---|---|---|---|---|---|
| | | | | | • | • | • | • | 27 |
| | | | | • | • | • | • | | 26 |
| | | | • | • | • | • | | | 25 |
| | | • | • | • | • | | | | 24 |
| | | • | • | • | • | | | | 23 |
| | | • | • | • | • | | | | 22 |
| | | | • | • | • | • | | | 21 |
| | | | • | • | • | • | | | 20 |
| | | | • | • | • | • | • | | 19 |
| • | • | • | • | • | | | | | 18 |
| | | | | | | | | | 17 |
| | | • | • | • | • | | | | 16 |
| | | | • | • | • | • | | | 15 |
| | | | • | • | • | • | | | 14 |
| | | • | • | • | • | • | | | 13 |
| | | • | • | • | • | | | | 12 |
| | • | • | • | • | | | | | 11 |
| • | • | • | • | | | | | | 10 |
| | | | | • | • | • | • | • | 9 |
| | | | • | • | • | • | | | 8 |
| | | • | • | • | • | | | | 7 |
| | • | • | • | • | | | | | 6 |
| | • | • | • | • | | | | | 5 |
| | • | • | • | • | | | | | 4 |
| | • | • | • | • | | | | | 3 |
| | | • | • | • | • | | | | 2 |
| | | | • | • | • | • | | | 1 |

8 7 6 5 4 3 2 1

## THUMB GUSSET Chart

Or follow Gusset A in the Gussets in Words section

| | | | | | | | | | | | | |
|---|---|---|---|---|---|---|---|---|---|---|---|---|
| • | | • | | • | | • | | • | | • | | • | | • | 14 |
| • | ← | | • | | • | | • | | • | | • | → | • | 13 |
| • | | • | | • | | • | | • | | • | | • | 12 |
| • | ⇐ | | • | | • | | • | | • | | ⇒ | • | 11 |
| • | | | • | | • | | • | | • | | | • | 10 |
| • | | | | • | | • | | • | | | | • | 9 |
| • | | | | • | | • | | • | | | | • | 8 |
| • | | | ⇐ | | • | | • | | ⇒ | | | • | 7 |
| • | | | | | • | | • | | | | | • | 6 |
| • | | | | ← | | • | | → | | | | • | 5 |
| • | | | | | • | | • | | | | | • | 4 |
| • | | | | ⇐ | | • | | ⇒ | | | | • | 3 |
| • | | | | | | • | | | | | | • | 2 |
| ← | | | | | | • | | | | | | → | 1 |

## CHART SYMBOLS

• K1D    Empty square = K1L

← Make 1 Left with D    → Make 1 Right with D

⇐ Make 1 Left with L    ⇒ Make 1 Right with L

## SALT AND PEPPER PATTERN (S&P)

**Round 1.** (K1D, K1L).

**Round 2.** (K1L, K1D).

Work charts from right to left, bottom to top.

Always carry D on the left (ahead) and L on the right to prevent streaks in work.

Instructions apply to both hands unless otherwise indicated.

## CAST ON

Cast on 36 stitches for the wrist. Divide evenly on 3 needles and join in a circle, being careful not to twist. Work 30 rounds of (K2, P1) ribbing, or desired length, in a striped pattern of your choice.

**Increase Round.** Knit 1 round, increasing 13 stitches evenly spaced (49 stitches). Arrange work on needles: 24, 13, 12 stitches.

**Set-Up. Round 1. Right Hand.** Join new colour, and keeping D ahead (on the left) throughout, work stitches 1–8 of Seesaw Sea Round 1 chart three times. These 24 stitches form the front of the mitten. **Palm.** K1D, K1L, place marker. Make 1 right-leaning stitch with D, K1D. Make 1 left-leaning stitch with D, place marker. (K1L, K1D) to end of round.

Note that some thumb gusset rounds produce two or more adjacent stitches of the same colour. This is corrected on the following round. Follow Gusset A in Thumb Gussets in Words instead of the Thumb Gusset chart if preferred.

**Set-Up. Round 1. Left Hand.** Join new colour and, keeping D on the left (ahead) throughout, work Round 1 of Seesaw Sea chart three times (24 stitches for front). **Palm.** (K1D, K1L) until 3 stitches remain in round, place marker. Make 1 right-leaning stitch with D, K1D. Make 1 left-leaning stitch with D, place marker. K1L, K1D.

**Both Hands.** This sets up Seesaw Sea on the front, S&P stitches on the palm, and Round 1 of the thumb gusset between the markers.

**Set-Up. Round 2. Both Hands.** Work Seesaw Sea Round 2 on front. **Palm.** Work in S&P to marker, slip marker. Work Round 2 of Thumb Gusset chart (or use Gusset A in Gussets in Words) to next marker, slip marker. Work S&P to end of round.

Continue working successive rounds of patterns as established until thumb gusset Round 14 is complete, finishing the round in S&P. There will be 15 gusset stitches between markers.

**Next Round.** Work next round of Seesaw Sea on front. **Palm.** Work S&P to marker, remove marker. Place gusset stitches on a piece of waste yarn, remove marker. Cast on 1 stitch with D to bridge gap. Work S&P to end of round (49 stitches). Thumb gusset is complete.

Continue working Seesaw Sea on the front and S&P on the palm until 27 Seesaw Sea rounds are complete, finishing the round in S&P.

**Next Round.** Beginning with K1L, work 1 round in S&P.

Work 9 rounds more in S&P, or until work reaches the tip of the little finger.

**Shape Top**

To create the picket-fence top, use Two-Step Shaping, as follows.

**Shaping Round 1. Front.** With Seesaw Sea facing, K1 in correct colour. SSK with the next colour in the sequence. Resume S&P on the next stitch (having made 2 adjacent stitches of the same colour). Work in S&P until 3 stitches remain on front. K2tog in the same colour as the stitch just made. Work last stitch in correct colour of sequence. **Palm.** As front.

**Shaping Round 2. Front.** K1, SSK in next colour in the sequence. S&P until 3 stitches remain on front. K2tog in next colour in the sequence, K1. **Palm.** As front. Correct colour sequence is restored.

Repeat these 2 shaping rounds until 9 stitches remain. Break yarns, leaving a long tail. Thread tail into a needle and pass through remaining stitches knitwise. Pull tight and secure.

## THUMB

Transfer thumb stitches from holder to 2 double pointed needles. Rejoin yarns and knit these stitches in S&P. With another needle, pick up and knit 4 stitches in S&P at the base of the thumb (19 stitches). Note beginning of round. Work 12 rounds more in S&P, or until work reaches the tip of the thumb.

**Thumb Decrease Round 1.** (K1 with correct colour in the S&P sequence, SSK with next colour in the sequence, K1 in S&P), repeat to end of round working any leftover stitches in S&P.

**Thumb Decrease Round 2.** (K1 with correct S&P colour, SSK with next colour in the S&P sequence) to end of round working any leftover stitches in S&P. Break yarns. Thread through remaining stitches knitwise and secure.

## FINISHING

Press lightly with steam or under a damp cloth, avoiding ribbing.

© Shirley A. Scott 2024

Where it's wave over wave
Sea over bow
I'm as happy a man
As the sea will allow ...

Alan Doyle, "Wave over Wave"

# RIPPLE WRISTERS AND HEADBAND

**DEGREE OF DIFFICULTY** * **Smooth Sailing**

The swirls, eddies, bubbles, and surges that mark restless ocean tides are reflected in these Ripple Wristers. Dangerous whirlpools and dramatic waterspouts are also part of the fascinating turbulence that accompanies the movement of great waters.

> I have always disliked the sea, its surliness, its menace, its vast reaches and unknowable, shudder-inducing depths.
>
> John Banville, *The Untouchable*

The Old Sow whirlpool, which gets up to its tricks near the mouth of the Bay of Fundy between the coasts of New Brunswick and Maine, is the second largest in the world. It follows the Maelstrom in Norway and precedes Scotland's notorious Corryvreckan. A huge tide sweeps around the sharply angled tip of an island, while a strong current surges and the waters are forced into a deep ocean trench. Conditions are constantly changing but a vortex 75 metres in diameter has been observed.

Ripple Wristers are worked flat using a faux cable stitch that is fast and less bulky than true cables, with no cable needle needed. The wrist is gently shaped for a beautiful fit. The seam lies flat on the inner wrist. Optional bobbles help to identify the front when putting them on in a hurry. Replace them with small buttons if desired. Ripple Wristers make a sweet bridal accessory for cold weather weddings.

## SIZE

**Medium.** Circumference: 7.5 inches (19 cm), after pressing and seaming. Length: 10.25 inches (26 cm) from cast on to cast off.

## YOU NEED

200 metres of light worsted weight yarn (Group 3). Samples were knit with Briggs and Little Regal 100% wool.
Two 4.00 mm needles or a 4.00 mm circular needle.
Markers, row counter.

## GAUGE

24 stitches = 4 inches (10 cm) in stockinette.

## RIPPLE PATTERN

**M1 (Make 1)** by picking up the bar between 2 stitches, putting it on the left needle with the longer leg on the near side, then knitting into the back of this stitch.

**Make Bobble.** (Purl 1 into the front of the stitch, knit 1 into the back of the same stitch) twice, turn to wrong side of work, K4 bobble stitches. Turn to right side of work, P4 bobble stitches. On the working needle, pass the second, third, and fourth bobble stitches over the first bobble stitch, one by one.

**SSK (Slip Slip Knit).** Slip the next 2 stitches separately knitwise. Return them to the left needle and knit them together through the back of the loop.

**Increase 1 stitch purlwise** by purling into the front and back of the next stitch, making 2 purl stitches from 1.

## RIPPLE Chart

Chart shows right side rows only

| | | | | | | | |
|---|---|---|---|---|---|---|---|
| \ | | | M1 | | | | 15 |
| | \ | | | M1 | | | 13 |
| | | \ | | | M1 | | 11 |
| | | | | | | | 9 |
| | | M1 | | | / | | 7 |
| | M1 | | | / | | | 5 |
| M1 | | | / | | | | 3 |
| | | | | | | | 1 |

## CHART SYMBOLS

\ SSK      M1 = Make 1      / K2tog      Empty square = K1

## RIPPLE in Words

**Row 1.** Knit 6.

**Row 2 and all even numbered rows.** Knit the knits and purl the purls and M1 stitches.

**Row 3.** K2, K2tog, K2, M1.

**Row 5.** K1, K2tog, K2, M1, K1.

**Row 7.** K2tog, K2, M1, K2.

**Row 9.** K6.

**Row 11.** M1, K2, SSK, K2.

**Row 13.** K1, M1, K2, SSK, K1.

**Row 15.** K2, M1, K2, SSK.

Instructions for right and left hands are identical except for placement of the thumb gusset.

## CAST ON

Cast on 43 stitches. Knit 2 rows.

**Set-Up. Row 1. Right Side.** K3 border stitches, P2, K6, (P3, K6) three times, P2, K3 border stitches.

**Set-Up. Row 2. Wrong Side.** P3, K2, (P6, K3) three times, P6, K2, P3.

**Set-Up. Row 3.** K3 border, P2, (K6, P1, make bobble in next stitch, P1) three times, K6, P2, K3 border.

**Set-Up. Row 4.** P3, K2, (P6, K1, K2tog) three times, P6, K2, P3 (40 stitches).

## TIPS

Beginning a bobble on a purl stitch prevents holes at the base.

Wrong side rows where you knit the knits and purl the purls are called copy rows. They are relaxing.

When switching from knit stitches to purl stitches on the right side of the work, looseness may develop, as it sometimes does in cables and ribbing. To tighten up, insert needle in the purl stitch as usual but wrap the yarn around the needle from underneath the stitch (clockwise), instead of the usual way. This twists the purl stitch, tightening it up. On the following wrong side row, knit into the back of the stitch to correct the twist.

## HAND

Begin counting Ripple rows here.

**Row 1.** K3 border, stitches (work P2, Row 1 of Ripple) to last 5 stitches, P2, K3 border stitches. **Row 2.** P3, (K2, P6) to last 5 stitches, K2, P3.

Pattern is now established with 3 border stitches at the beginning and end of each row, and panels of Ripple separated by columns of purl stitches.

Beginning with Ripple Row 3, continue in patterns as set, working successive rows of Ripple between the purl stitches until Ripple Row 16 is complete.

Reset row counter to Row 1 here and after every following Row 16.

### Shape Wrist

**Row 1. Decrease Row.** With Ripple facing, K3 border, P2tog, (work Ripple Row 1, P2) three times, P2tog, K3 border (38 stitches).

**Row 2 and all even numbered rows.** Knit the knits and purl the purls.

**Row 3.** K3, P1, (work Ripple Row 3, P2) three times, Ripple Row 1, P1, K3.

Continue as established until Ripple Row 6 is complete.

**Ripple Row 7. Decrease Row.** K3, P1, Ripple Row 7, P2tog, Ripple Row 7, P2, Ripple Row 7, P2tog, Ripple Row 7, P1, K3 (36 stitches). Continue in pattern as established until Ripple Row 12 is complete.

**Row 13. Increase Row.** K3, P1, work Ripple Row 13, increase 1 stitch purlwise in the next stitch thereby making 2 purls out of 1, Ripple Row 13, P2, Ripple Row 13, increase 1 stitch purlwise in the next stitch, Ripple Row 13, P1, K3 (38 stitches). **Rows 14–16.** Continue in pattern as established.

**Ripple Row 1. Next Row. Increase Row.** K3, increase 1 stitch purlwise in the next stitch. Work (Ripple Row 1, P2) three times, Ripple Row 1, increase 1 stitch purlwise in the next stitch, K3 (40 stitches).

Continue in pattern as established until Ripple Row 8 is complete.

### Thumb Gusset

**Row 9. Gusset Increase Row. Right Hand.** K3, (P2, Ripple Row 9) three times, place marker. (Increase 1 stitch purlwise in the next stitch) twice, place marker. Work in pattern to end of row (4 purl stitches between markers).

**Row 9. Gusset Increase Row. Left Hand.** K3, P2, work Ripple Row 9 once, place marker. (Increase 1 stitch purlwise in the next stitch) twice, place marker. Work in pattern to end of row. The purl stitches between markers are now gusset stitches.

**Row 11. Gusset Increase Row.** Work established patterns with Ripple Row 11 to marker, slip marker. Increase 1 stitch purlwise in the next stitch, P2, increase 1 stitch purlwise in the next stitch, slip marker. Work in pattern to end of row (6 gusset stitches).

**Row 13. Gusset Increase Row.** Work in pattern with Ripple Row 13 to marker, slip marker. Increase 1 stitch purlwise in the next stitch, purl until 1 stitch remains before marker, increase 1 stitch purlwise in the next stitch, slip marker. Work in pattern to end of row (8 gusset stitches).

Continue in pattern, working successive rows of Ripple and increasing the number of gusset stitches by repeating Gusset Rows 13 and 14 between markers until there are 12 gusset stitches, ending with Ripple Row 2.

**Row 3.** Work pattern to marker, remove marker. P1 gusset stitch. Cast off next 10 gusset stitches loosely purlwise. Remove marker. This leaves 2 purl stitches on right needle. Work in pattern to the end of the row. Gusset is complete.

**Row 4.** Knit the knits and purl the purls, tightening up the gusset opening. There is no need to cast on a stitch to bridge the gap. Continue in pattern until Ripple Row 16 is complete.

### Top Border

**Next Row.** K1, K2tog, (P2, K2) to last 3 stitches, K2tog, K1. Work 3 rows more in ribbing. Cast off in rib.

### FINISHING

Press lightly with steam on wrong side before seaming, paying particular attention to the selvages. Flat selvages make sewing easier. Sew seam with right side facing using mattress stitch.

© Shirley A. Scott 2024

## BIG SPLASH TRIVIA

### SKP or SSK?

Both slip, knit, pass (SKP) and slip, slip, knit (SSK) are left-leaning decreases. You will often find them in partnership with K2tog, the usual right-leaning decrease. SKP and SSK do the same job. What is the difference between them?

They are interchangeable, but SSK has a neater appearance. A diagonal line of SSKs in a raglan sweater, for example, is a marvel. Some people prefer to make an even tidier SSK by slipping the second stitch purlwise, not knitwise. Try it!

SKP, formerly known as slip 1, K1, psso, is a good choice for lace knitting. When paired with a yarnover, it creates a bigger hole than SSK makes. This is desirable in lace.

The principle behind all knitting decreases is to create a sandwich of stitches. The stitch that the working needle touches first to make the sandwich will always end up on the top of the stack.

## TIP Mattress Stitch

Here are some simple instructions. Excellent videos are widely available.

These instructions apply when working upward, away from ribbing. Hold selvage edges together, right side facing. Insert needle into the centre of the long stitch in selvage on the right, pass under the knot and up in the middle of the next long stitch above it.

Insert needle in corresponding stitch of selvage on the left, draw yarn through to the right side in the same way as the right edge.

When drawing yarn through to the right side, don't pull it tight. Work from edge to edge in this manner, matching rows and keeping the seam elastic.

# RIPPLE HEADBAND

Need warm ears and something to match your Ripple Wristers fast? This headband is knit flat on two needles and quickly seamed. It makes efficient use of oddments of yarn. And unless you are protecting a very expensive hairdo, be sure that your headband fits snugly because it will stretch gently when worn.

## SIZE

Length: 18 inches (46 cm) unstretched. Depth: 3.25 inches (8.5 cm). For custom sizes, add or subtract stitches in groups of 8. For a deeper headband, add more rows of ribbing.

## YOU NEED

50 metres light worsted weight yarn (Group 3), or an oddment. Samples were knit with Briggs and Little Regal 100% wool. Two 4.00 mm needles.

## GAUGE

22.5 stitches = 4 inches (10 cm) in pattern.

## CAST ON

Cast on 96 stitches. Work 3 rows in (K1, P1) ribbing.

**Row 1. Right Side.** P1, K6, (P2, K6) to last stitch, P1.

**Row 2 and all even numbered rows.** K1, (P6, K2) to last 7 stitches, P6, K1.

**Row 3.** P1, K2, K2tog, K2, make 1, (P2, K2, K2tog, K2, make 1) to last stitch, P1.

**Row 5.** P1, K1, K2tog, K2, make 1, K1, (P2, K1, K2tog, K2, make 1, K1) to last 7 stitches, K1, K2tog, K2, make 1, K1, P1.

**Row 7.** P1, K2tog, K2, make 1, K2, (P2, K2tog, K2, make 1, K2) to last 3 stitches, K2, P1.

**Row 9.** As Row 1.

**Row 11.** P1, make 1, K2, SSK, K2, (P2, make 1, K2, SSK, K2), P1.

**Row 13.** P1, K1, make 1, K2, SSK, K1, (P2, K1, make 1, K2, SSK, K1), P1.

**Row 15.** P1, K2, make 1, K2, SSK, (P2, K2, make 1, K2, SSK), P1.

**Row 16.** As Row 2.

Beginning with P1, work 3 rows in (K1, P1) ribbing. Cast off loosely in rib.

**FINISHING**

Do not press or block. With right side facing, sew ends together.

© Shirley A. Scott 2024

# JIGS AND REELS
## Trigger Mitts

## DEGREE OF DIFFICULTY *** Gale Force

This handsome abstract pattern makes a large, intriguing trigger mitt. The construction is challenging but detailed step-by-step instructions will guide you. The stitch pattern is quick to knit, with little weaving on the back. It's easily learned and very, very warm. A great work mitten!

## SIZE

**Large.** Circumference: 10 inches (25.5 cm). Length from beginning of Jigs and Reels pattern: 7.5 inches (19 cm). Length of thumb and trigger finger is adjustable.

## YOU NEED

Two shades of light worsted weight yarn (Group 3): 125 metres of Dark (D) and 125 metres of Light (L). Samples were knit with Briggs and Little Regal 100% wool. 1 set of 4.00 mm double pointed needles. 2 thinner double pointed needles for trigger mitt bind off only (optional). Ring markers.

## GAUGE

24 stitches and 28 rows = 4 inches (10 cm).

## JIGS AND REELS Chart

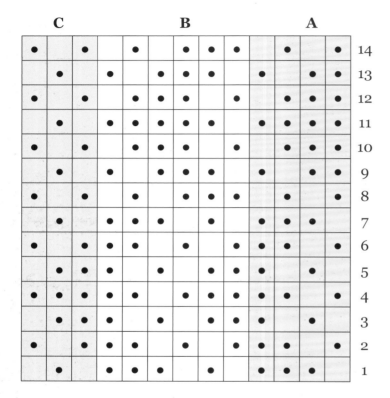

## THUMB GUSSET Chart

Use Gusset A in Thumb Gussets in Words if preferred

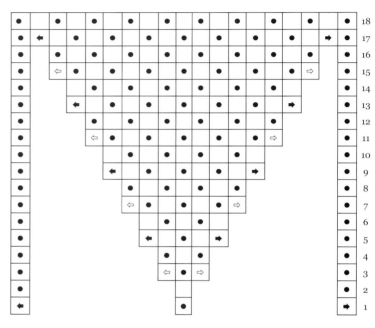

## CHART SYMBOLS

● K1D

Empty square = K1L

➡ Make 1 Right with D

⬅ Make 1 Left with D

⇦ Make 1 Left with L

⇨ Make 1 Right with L

## SALT AND PEPPER PATTERN (S&P)

**Round 1.** (K1D, K1L).
**Round 2.** (K1L, K1D).

Charts are worked from right to left, bottom to top.

Always carry D ahead on the left to prevent streaks in colour work.

Instructions pertain to both right and left hands unless otherwise indicated.

Note that when creating the thumb gusset there may be 2 or more adjacent stitches of the same colour on some rounds. This is corrected on the following round.

## CAST ON

Cast on 42 stitches and join in a circle, being careful not to twist. Work 30 rounds in (K2, P1) ribbing or desired length in a striped pattern of your choice.

**Next Round.** Knit, increasing 17 stitches evenly spaced, 59 stitches. Arrange 31 stitches on a single needle for the front of the mitten. Divide remaining stitches conveniently on 2 needles for the palm.

## HAND

**Set-Up. Round 1. Right Hand. Front.** Join contrast colour and work section A of Jigs and Reels chart once. Work section

## TIPS

If you're unsure about length, try completing the thumb before putting the trigger finger stitches on a holder. Finishing the thumb at this point makes it easier to determine the correct hand length before beginning the trigger finger.

After finishing the thumb gusset and putting its stitches on a holder, work a few rounds in pattern as directed. Then put the thumb stitches on double pointed needles and the hand stitches on holders. Work the thumb and return the hand stitches to double pointed needles.

B of Jigs and Reels four times. Work section C of Jigs and Reels once. **Palm.** K1D, K1L, place marker. Make 1 right-leaning stitch with D, K1D. Make 1 left-leaning stitch with D, place marker. (K1L, K1D) to last stitch, K1L. The stitches between the markers are Round 1 of the Thumb Gusset chart.

**Round 1. Left Hand. Front.** Join L and work section A of Jigs and Reels once. Work section B of Jigs and Reels four times. Work section C of Jigs and Reels once. These 31 stitches form the front of the mitten. **Palm.** (K1D, K1L) until 4 stitches remain in round. Place marker. Make 1 right-leaning stitch with D, K1D. Make 1 left-leaning stitch with D. Place marker. K1L, K1D, K1L.

The pattern is now established. There are Jigs and Reels stitches on the front, S&P stitches on the palm, with thumb gusset stitches between the markers on the palm. Use Gusset A in the Thumb Gussets in Words section instead of the Thumb Gusset chart if preferred.

Continue working consecutive rounds of Jigs and Reels on the front, S&P on the palm, and the thumb gusset between the markers on the palm until Round 18 of the thumb gusset is complete. Finish the round in S&P.

**Next Round.** Work next round of Jigs and Reels on front. **Palm.** Work S&P to marker, remove marker. Place 19 gusset stitches on a piece of waste yarn, remove marker. Cast on 1

stitch with correct colour of S&P to bridge gap. Work S&P to end of round (59 stitches). Thumb gusset is complete.

Continue working Jigs and Reels on the front and S&P on the palm until 28 rounds of Jigs and Reels are complete on the front. Finish the round in S&P.

**Next Round.** Beginning with K1L, work 2 or more rounds in S&P. Read the tip about completing the thumb. If extra hand length is needed, continue in S&P to the point where fingers begin. **Left Hand Only.** Break yarns.

**Next Round. Both Hands. Reserve Trigger Finger Stitches.** With Jigs and Reels facing, at the same edge of the mitten as the thumb, place 8 stitches from the front and corresponding 8 stitches from the palm on holders for the trigger finger.

**Next Round. Right Hand.** With Jigs and Reels facing, work in S&P to the gap. Cast on 2 stitches in pattern to bridge gap. Work in S&P to end of round (45 stitches).

**Next Round. Left Hand.** With Jigs and Reels facing, rejoin yarns at stitch 9 of the front. This is the new beginning of round. Work S&P on the front and palm to the gap. Cast on 2 stitches in pattern to bridge gap. Work in S&P to end of round (45 stitches).

**Both Hands.** Work 13 rounds more in S&P or until the work reaches the tip of the little finger. **Both Hands.** Arrange stitches on needles as follows. Place the first 22 stitches of the front on a single needle. Divide the remaining 23 palm stitches on 2 needles.

**Shape Top.** Shape the top of the mitten using the Three-Step Shaping, as follows.

**Decrease Round 1. Front.** With Jigs and Reels facing, K1 in correct colour. SSK with the next colour in the sequence. Resume S&P on the next stitch (having made 2 adjacent stitches of the same colour). Work in pattern until 3 stitches remain on front. K2tog in the same colour as the stitch just made. Work last stitch in correct colour. **Palm.** As front.

**Decrease Round 2. Front.** K1, SSK in next colour in the sequence. S&P until 3 stitches remain on front. K2tog in next colour in the sequence, K1. **Palm.** As front. Correct colour sequence is restored.

**Decrease Round 3.** Work in S&P without decreasing.

Repeat this three-step sequence twice more (21 stitches). Break yarns, leaving a long tail in the last stitch to work the bind off.

**Three-Needle Bind Off.** The hand is finished with a Three-Needle Bind Off on the wrong side of the work.

Place stitches of front on a length of waste yarn. Place stitches of palm on another length of yarn. Turn mitten inside out to work bind off on the wrong side using the long tail.

Return stitches on holders to 2 thinner double pointed needles for easier working. Hold these needles parallel to one another, the needle with the larger number of stitches nearest you. With a third double pointed needle and the long tail, K1 from the front holding needle. Then knit 1 stitch from this needle together with 1 stitch of the opposite colour from the rear needle: 2 stitches now on the working needle. Pass first stitch on working needle over second stitch to cast it off. 1 stitch remains on working needle. Continue to knit together 1 stitch from front and rear holding needles and slipping the first stitch over second stitch on the working needle to cast off. Repeat until 1 stitch remains on working needle. Fasten off and darn ends. Turn work right side out.

## THUMB

Transfer thumb stitches from holder to 2 double pointed needles. Rejoin yarns and knit these stitches in S&P. With another needle, pick up and knit 2 stitches in S&P at the base of the thumb (21 stitches). Note beginning of round. Work 15 rounds more in S&P, or until work reaches the tip of the thumb. Work Finger Decrease Rounds 1–2.

## TRIGGER FINGER

Transfer reserved stitches from front to a double pointed needle. Place corresponding stitches from palm on another double pointed needle.

**Next Round. Right Trigger Finger.** With Jigs and Reels facing, rejoin yarns and work in S&P to the gap. Pick up and knit 5 stitches in correct S&P sequence from the base of the hand (21 stitches).

**Next Round. Left Trigger Finger.** With Jigs and Reels facing, rejoin yarns, working stitches of front in S&P. Pick up and knit 5 stitches in correct colour sequence from base of hand. Work palm stitches in S&P (21 stitches).

**Next Round. Both Hands.** Note beginning of round. Divide stitches on 3 double pointed needles and work 17 rounds more in S&P, or until work reaches the tip of the index finger.

**Finger Decrease Round 1.** (K1 with correct colour in the S&P sequence, SSK with next colour in the sequence, K1 in S&P), repeat to end of round working any leftover stitches in S&P. Adjacent stitches in the same colour will be eliminated in the next round.

**Finger Decrease Round 2.** (K1 with correct S&P colour, SSK with next colour in the S&P sequence) to end of round, working any leftover stitches in S&P. Break yarns. Thread through remaining stitches and secure.

**FINISHING.** Darn ends securely. Press lightly, omitting ribbing.

© Shirley A. Scott 2024

# DOWNSHORE CLASSIC MITTENS
## An Old Home Memory

**DEGREE OF DIFFICULTY** * * * **Gale Force**

Childhood memories grow stronger as the years go by. When we were on long summer visits to our old home on the Bay Chaleur, we often breathed the quiet peace of evenings such as these by the water. Downshore, where our roots run deep, the land rises to high banks above the bay. In those days, when farming was the way of life, the bank fields were fenced and used as pasture.

This design records a sweet and soothing memory of deep home. Looking out over the water, the sun sets softly, while birds return to roost in the little woods nearby, silhouetted against sky and sea.

Here's an opportunity to knit this experience with as few as two colours, as many as six, or any number in between. The dark pattern colour remains the same throughout, while the background may remain the same, or change to reflect the mood of sky and sea.

**SIZE**

**Medium.** Circumference: 8.5 inches (21.5 cm). Length from cast on to cast off: 10.5 inches (27.5 cm), or desired length.

**YOU NEED**

**Sunset Version.** Small amounts of six shades of light worsted weight wool (Group 3). Samples were knit with less than 50 metres each of Briggs and Little Regal 100% wool in Midnight Blue (dark blue), Quoddy Blue (medium blue), Horizon Blue (light blue), and Briar Rose (pink). Very small amounts of Forest Brown (light brown) and Copper (amber) were also used.

**Two-Colour Version.** 100 metres each of two shades of light worsted weight yarn (Group 3). Samples were knit with Briggs and Little Regal 100% wool.

One set of 4.00 mm double pointed needles. Markers.

**GAUGE**

22 stitches x 24 rows = 4 inches (10 cm).

## DOWNSHORE Right Hand

**Sunset Version. Pattern colour (D):** dark blue. **Background colours (L):** Rounds 1–3: medium blue. 4–15: light blue. 16: light brown. 17–19: amber. 20–31: pink. 32–34: amber. 35: light brown.

Digits indicate the number of background stitches before the next pattern stitch.

... There midnight's all a'glimmer
And noon a purple glow
And evening full of the linnet's wings.

W.B. Yeats, "The Lake Isle of Innisfree"

Chart (digits indicate number of background stitches before the next pattern stitch; read with row numbers 1–35 at right):

| Row | Digits (left → right) |
|---|---|
| 35 | |
| 34 | 7, 5 |
| 33 | 9, 6 |
| 32 | 15, 7 |
| 31 | 7, 7 |
| 30 | 6, 8 |
| 29 | 6, 5 |
| 28 | 5, 5 |
| 27 | 5 |
| 26 | 5, 10 |
| 25 | 6, 11, 5 |
| 24 | 9, 10 |
| 23 | 13 |
| 22 | 9, 5 |
| 21 | 5, 7, 8 |
| 20 | 9, 9 |
| 19 | 7, 14 |
| 18 | 15 |
| 17 | 8 |
| 16 | 12, 6 |
| 15 | 10, 12 |
| 14 | 7, 11 |
| 13 | 12 |
| 12 | 8 |
| 11 | |
| 10 | 6, 5 |
| 9 | 6, 6 |
| 8 | 6 |
| 7 | 11 |
| 6 | 10 |
| 5 | 5 |
| 4 | |
| 3 | |
| 2 | |
| 1 | |

# DOWNSHORE Left Hand

**Sunset Version. Pattern colour (D):** dark blue.

**Background colours (L):** Rounds 1–3: medium blue. 4–15: light blue. 16: light brown. 17–19: amber. 20–31: pink. 32–34: amber. 35: light brown.

## THUMB GUSSET Chart

Or follow Gusset A in Gussets in Words

*(Thumb Gusset chart: a triangular grid of 14 rows, numbered 14 down to 1 on the right side, with dots indicating K1D pattern colour, empty squares for K1L background colour, and directional arrows for the increase stitches.)*

## CHART SYMBOLS

- • K1D pattern colour

  Empty square = K1L background colour

➡ Make 1 Right with D     ⬅ Make 1 Left with D

⇨ Make 1 Right with L     ⇦ Make 1 Left with L

**Digits** refer to the number of Light background stitches before the next Dark pattern stitch.

## SALT AND PEPPER PATTERN (S&P)

**Round 1.** (K1D, K1L).

**Round 2.** (K1L, K1D).

Instructions are for both hands unless otherwise noted.

Charts for left and right hand are different for the front of the mitten. Thumb Gusset chart is the same for both hands.

Work charts from right to left, bottom to top.

Weave unused colours in frequently on long stretches of a single colour.

Always carry the dark pattern colour on the left (ahead) and the light background colour on the right. This prevents streaks in the work.

Note that some thumb gusset rounds will produce adjacent stitches of the same colour. This is corrected on the following round.

## CAST ON

With desired wrist colour, cast on 36 stitches. Join in a circle, being careful not to twist and divide work evenly on 3 double pointed needles. Work 25–30 rounds in (K2, P1) striped ribbing in colours of choice.

**Increase Round.** Knit, increasing 13 stitches evenly spaced (49 stitches). Arrange stitches on needles: 25, 12, 12.

## BIG SPLASH TRIVIA

### Two- or Three-Step Shaping?

Salt and Pepper (S&P) pattern, the backbone of so many traditional designs, has its own rules. Decreases, for example, require at least 2 rounds to complete. The first round disrupts the sequence and the second round brings everything back to normal. You can never simply sneak in a K2tog when you need one.

**Two-Step Shaping** requires 2 rounds. Decreases on the first round interrupt the S&P. Decreases on the second round restore the pattern. It is used on mittens with a picket-fence top, the toe of our Big Holiday Stocking, or anywhere that a steep and steady angle of decrease is desired. It is finished off by threading the remaining loops of the last round with the tail of yarn, pulling tight and securing.

**Three-Step Shaping** requires 3 rounds. The first 2 rounds are the same as in Two-Step Shaping. The third round is worked with no decreases of any kind. This relaxes the decrease angle and creates the gentler shaping of round top mittens with their generous finger room, and adds flexibility to the ankle shaping on vamps. It is usually finished off by grafting in Kitchener stitch or that *ne plus ultra* of fine finishes, the Three-Needle Bind Off.

### Set-Up. Right Hand

**Round 1. Front.** Work Round 1 of Downshore Right Hand chart on first 25 stitches of the round. These stitches form the front of the mitten. **Palm.** K1 with L, K1 with D, K1 with L. Place marker. Work Round 1 of thumb gusset as follows. Make 1 right-leaning stitch with D, K1D, make 1 left-leaning stitch with D. Place marker. Work (K1L, K1D) to end of round.

**Round 2. Front.** Work Round 2 of Downshore on first 25 stitches of round. **Palm.** K1D, K1L, K1D. Slip marker. Work Round 2 of thumb gusset from the chart or from written instructions. Slip marker. Work (K1D, K1L) to end of round.

### Set-Up. Left Hand

**Round 1. Front.** Work Round 1 of Downshore Left Hand chart on first 25 stitches of round. These stitches form the front of the mitten. **Palm.** (K1L, K1D) until 3 stitches remain in round. Place marker. Make 1 right-leaning stitch with D, K1D. Make 1 left-leaning stitch with D. Place marker. K1L, K1D.

**Round 2. Front.** Work Round 2 of Downshore on first 25 stitches of round. **Palm.** (K1D, K1L) to marker. Slip marker. Work Round 2 of thumb gusset from chart or from written instructions. Slip marker. K1D, K1L.

## Both Hands

This establishes the Downshore pattern on the front of the mitten, S&P on the palm outside of the markers, and thumb gusset between the markers.

Continue working successive rounds of Downshore from the correct chart on the front, S&P on the palm, and thumb gusset between markers, until Round 14 is complete.

**Round 15. Front.** Work Round 15 of Downshore. **Palm.** Work S&P to marker, remove marker. Slip thumb gusset stitches to a piece of waste yarn, remove marker. Cast on 1 stitch with D to bridge the gap. Work S&P to end of round.

Continue working Downshore on the front and S&P on the palm until Round 35 is complete, working the palm in S&P.

**Sunset Only.** Break L and join light blue on the next round.

## Shape Top

Note that some shaping rounds will produce adjacent stitches of the same colour. This is corrected in the following round.

Work 4 rounds more of S&P or until work reaches the tip of the little finger.

Shape top using Three-Step Shaping, as follows.

**Shaping Round 1. Front.** With Downshore facing, K1 in correct colour. SSK with the next colour in the sequence. Resume S&P on the next stitch (having made 2 adjacent stitches of the same colour). Work in S&P until 3 stitches remain on front. K2tog in the same colour as the stitch just made. Work last stitch in correct colour of sequence. **Palm.** As front.

**Shaping Round 2. Front.** K1, SSK in next colour in the sequence. S&P until 3 stitches remain on front. K2tog in next colour in the sequence, K1. **Palm.** As front. Correct colour sequence is restored.

**Shaping Round 3.** Work in S&P to end of round without decreasing.

Repeat these 3 shaping rounds three times more (17 stitches). Arrange stitches on needles: 8, 4, 5. Break yarns, leaving a long tail of one colour.

For a smoothly rounded top, the mitten is finished with a Three-Needle Bind Off on the wrong side of the work.

Place 8 front stitches on a piece of waste yarn. Place 9 palm stitches on another piece of waste yarn. Turn mitten inside out to bind off.

Return stitches to 2 double pointed needles. Have the needle with the greater number of stitches nearest you. With a third needle (a thinner double pointed needle is useful but optional), K1 from the front needle with the long tail.

Now knit together 1 stitch from the front holding nee-

dle together with 1 stitch of the opposite colour from the back holding needle. There are now 2 stitches on the working needle. Pass first stitch on working needle over second stitch, thereby casting it off. 1 stitch remains on working needle.

Continue to knit together 1 stitch of each colour from front and back needles, then slipping the first stitch over second stitch on the working needle to cast off. Repeat until 1 stitch remains. Break yarn, thread through loop and secure. Turn mitten to right side. Do not poke out the corners. Keep it rounded.

### THUMB

Transfer thumb gusset stitches to 2 needles. Join dark and light yarns (use light blue if working Sunset) and work thumb stitches in S&P. Pick up and knit 4 stitches at the base of the thumb in correct S&P order (19 stitches). Note beginning of round.

Do 12 more rounds in S&P, or until work reaches the tip of the thumb. Change background colours as follows if working Sunset.

### Sunset Only

1 round dark blue and light blue.
1 round dark blue and light brown.
3 rounds dark blue and amber.
7 rounds, or desired length, in dark blue and pink.

**Thumb Decrease Round 1.** (K1 with correct S&P colour. K2tog with next colour in the S&P sequence. K1 S&P). Repeat to end of round, knitting last 3 stitches in S&P (15 stitches).

**Thumb Decrease Round 2.** (K1 S&P, K2tog in S&P) to end of round, working last 3 stitches in S&P (12 stitches). Break yarns, thread through remaining stitches knitwise and secure.

### FINISHING

Darn ends securely. Press mitten well with steam or under a damp cloth. Do not press ribbing.

© Shirley A. Scott 2024

# THERMAL CAP
## in Knit and Purl Stitches

**DEGREE OF DIFFICULTY** * Smooth Sailing

Knit and purl patterns are a joy to work. These two stitches, the building blocks of our world, combine in hundreds of different ways, from simple to audacious. In this easy design, they create a cozy thermal effect, a great thing to tuck in your pocket for a walk in the woods or for working outdoors. This is an ear-warming, close fitting hat with a choice of bands and sizes. Interesting octagonal crown shaping creates a gently rounded top.

## SIZE

**Small/Medium.** Circumference: 18 inches (45.5 cm). Length from cast on to cast off: 8 inches (20 cm), or as desired. Crown shaping: 2.5 inches (6 cm). This cap stretches easily to 20 inches (51 cm) but with a snug fit.

**Medium/Large.** Circumference: 22 inches (55.5 cm). Length from cast on to cast off: 8.5 inches (22 cm), or as desired. Crown shaping: 3 inches (7.5 cm). A relaxed fit for Medium, snug for Large.

Change gauge for custom sizes.

## YOU NEED

100 metres of light worsted weight yarn (Group 3). Samples were knit in Briggs and Little Regal 100% wool.

One set of 4.00 mm double pointed needles. A set of five needles makes crown shaping easier. Cap may also be knit on a 4.00 mm circular needle, switching to double points when work becomes tight.

Markers.

## GAUGE

20 stitches = 4 inches (10 cm) in Thermal pattern.

## THERMAL PATTERN

**Round 1.** Knit.
**Round 2.** (K1, P1).

Instructions are given for S/M (those for M/L follow in parentheses). If only one instruction appears, it applies to both sizes.

## CAST ON

Cast on 96 (104) stitches. Join in a circle, being careful not to twist. Place marker to indicate beginning of round.

**Ribbed Band.** Work 1 inch (2.5 cm) or desired length in K2, P2 ribbing. **Roll Up Band.** Knit every round for 1 inch (2.5 cm), or desired length. Purl 1 round.

Repeat the 2 rounds of Thermal until work measures 6 (7) inches (15, 17.5 cm) or desired length before crown shaping, ending with Round 1, a knit round.

Crown shaping will add 2.5 inches (6 cm) to S/M cap, 3 inches (7.5 cm) to M/L. For a slouchy look, lengthen cap here first.

Work Thermal Round 2, placing a marker after every 12 (13) stitches. This divides the crown into 8 segments.

Switch to double pointed needles if needed when work becomes tight.

## SHAPE CROWN
### Size S/M Only

**Shaping Round 1. Decrease Round.** In each segment, knit until 2 stitches remain before marker, K2tog, slip marker.

**Shaping Round 2.** (K1, P1) until 2 stitches remain before marker, K2, slip marker.

### Rounded Top or Pointed Top?

The fewer segments in the crown shaping of a hat, the more pointed the top will be, whereas dividing the crown into lots of equal segments means a faster finish and a gentler shaping. Imagine two hats that have the same number of stitches. It will require more decrease rounds to reach the summit if there are 5 segments, fewer if there are 8.

It is also a good idea to decrease on every round when you get very near the top to avoid a point. Happily, unwanted points can always be hidden by pompoms. Experienced knitters sew a button to the inside of the cap at the top so the pompom can be easily changed to match an outfit.

The frequency of decrease rounds can certainly affect the shape. With the exception of unusual hats such as the pillbox, the crown of most that we make is decreased on every second round. But the crown of the distinctive Peruvian chullo, for example, is decreased every second round until half the stitches remain, then on every round until half of those remain again, as on the toe of a sock. Its finished shape is a rounded pyramid, designed to fold over in a jaunty way. The world of knitting is vast.

And then there were the Useful Presents: engulfing mufflers of the old coach days, and mittens made for giant sloths ... bunny-suited busbies and balaclavas for victims of head-shrinking tribes ...

Dylan Thomas, *A Child's Christmas in Wales*

**Shaping Round 3. Decrease Round.** As Shaping Round 1.

**Shaping Round 4.** (K1, P1) to last stitch before marker, K1, slip marker.

Repeat these 4 shaping rounds until 4 stitches remain in each segment, ending with a knit round.

**Next Round.** (K1, P1, K2tog, slip marker) to end of round (32 stitches).

**Next Round.** (K1, K2tog), removing markers as you come to them (24 stitches).

**Next Round.** K2tog to end of round (12 stitches).

**Size M/L Only**

**Set-Up Round.** Knit until 3 stitches remain before marker, K2tog, K1, slip marker. Repeat to end of round.

**Shaping Round 1.** [(K1, P1) until 2 stitches remain before marker, K2, slip marker. (P1, K1) until 3 stitches remain before next marker, K2, P1, slip marker].

Repeat [ to ] three times more.

**Shaping Round 2. Decrease Round.** (Knit until 3 stitches remain before marker, K2tog, K1, slip marker. Knit until 4 stitches remain before next marker, K2tog, K2, slip marker).

Repeat (to) three times more.

**Shaping Round 3.** [(K1, P1) until 3 stitches remain before marker, K3, slip marker. (P1, K1) until 3 stitches remain before next marker, K2, P1, slip marker.]

Repeat [ to ] three times more.

**Shaping Round 4. Decrease Round.** As Round 2. Repeat these 4 shaping rounds until there are 32 stitches on the needles (4 stitches remain in each segment).

Work Shaping Round 3.

**Next Round.** Removing markers as you come to them, (K1, K2tog, K1, K2tog, K2) to end of round (24 stitches).

**Next Round.** K2tog to end of round (12 stitches).

**Both Sizes.** Break yarn. Thread through remaining loops knitwise and secure.

**FINISHING**

Press lightly with steam or a damp cloth.

© Shirley A. Scott 2024

## Stretching Caps to Fit

Knit hats should always feel a little tight at first. As time passes, woollen head gear stretches gently to fit the head of the wearer, and it stays stretched. But not everyone has the patience to wait. Here's how to speed things up in a crisis.

First, find a suitable household object the same circumference as your head. This can become a challenge equal to a scavenger hunt. Professional milliners have wooden forms. Others have purchased glass or foam heads. We once had a glass rose bowl that worked perfectly when upside down. Be inventive. An inflated balloon is not recommended.

Soak your garment in warm water for 10 minutes. When it is thoroughly wet, it will temporarily become very stretchy. Ease the hat onto the form, as with sock stretchers, and leave it to dry. It must be completely warm to the touch before you remove it. A damp cap will be cool to the touch and will shrink to its original size when dry. Check the inside surface as well as the outside.

If the search for a household object proves fruitless, here's a last resort. Wear the wet hat until it dries completely. Unpleasant for a while perhaps, but it is guaranteed to keep its new shape forever. Some military berets are custom-fitted this way.

### Cap Too Large?

In this crisis, felting springs immediately to mind. Beware. Felting might work occasionally for knitters born under a lucky star, but the process is uncertain and hard to control. The number of unknowns is huge—the properties of the fibre, twist of the yarn, water temperature, speed of agitation, etc. More importantly, felting tends to shrink garments to a short and fat shape, not proportionately. It's dicey.

Our suggestion is to buy or make a liner to sew in. Sometimes an inexpensive hat purchased from a bargain store does the trick. Sometimes custom lining is needed. People who find wool itchy to wear truly appreciate this solution. Or it's back to the needles and try again.

# THERMAL MITTS
## in Knit and Purl Stitches

**DEGREE OF DIFFICULTY * Smooth Sailing**

This cozy mitten is a workhorse. The textured stitch pattern is warm yet stretchy, so one size fits many hands. There's even room for another mitt underneath. The top shaping is generous enough for wide hands and the length is adjustable. Although not precisely symmetrical, right and left hands are almost identical, so make two the same. Second Mitt Syndrome will never be a problem.

Take time to appreciate the artistry of this seamless design. Even the palm and thumb are patterned. With alternate rounds of rib and easy knit stitches, it's definitely smooth sailing.

## SIZE

**Medium/Large.** Circumference: 8.5 inches (21.5 cm) without stretching. This size will fit many hands. Length from beginning of Thermal pattern to cast off: 7 inches (18 cm), or as desired.

For custom sizes, change gauge.

## YOU NEED

150 metres of light worsted weight yarn (Group 3). Samples were knit with Briggs and Little Regal 100% wool.

One set of 4.00 mm double pointed needles. Markers.

## GAUGE

22 stitches = 4 inches (10 cm) in Thermal pattern.

## THERMAL PATTERN

**Round 1.** (K1, P1) to end of round.
**Round 2.** Knit to end of round.

## Thumb Gusset

**Round 1.** Make 1, K3, make 1 (5 stitches).

**Round 2.** (K1, P1) two times, K1.

**Round 3.** Make 1, K5, make 1.

**Round 4.** (P1, K1) three times, P1.

**Round 5.** Make 1, K7, make 1.

**Round 6.** (K1, P1) four times, K1.

**Round 7.** Make 1, K9, make 1.

**Round 8.** (P1, K1) five times, P1.

**Round 9.** Make 1, K11, make 1.

**Round 10.** (K1, P1) six times, K1 (13 stitches).

Read about increasing before beginning thumb gusset.

Note that some thumb gusset rounds will produce two or more adjacent knit stitches.

## CAST ON

Cast on 36 stitches. Join in a round, being careful not to twist. Work desired length in (K2, P2) ribbing, increasing 6 stitches evenly spaced on last round (42 stitches).

Arrange stitches on needles: 14, 14, 14.

**Set-Up. Next Round.** K19, place marker, K3, place marker, knit to end of round. Stitches inside markers are the base of the thumb gusset.

## TIP Thumb Gusset Increases

The birthing of new stitches within thumb gusset markers is always tricky but choosing a method is easier if using a single colour. Which increase is best?

In days gone by, the standard increase in patterns was knitting into the front and back of a stitch. It's the first method that most of us learned and it works well in some circumstances, but it also creates an undesirable little bump at the base of the newborn stitch.

For single colour mittens such as this, make one stitch in the thumb gusset by picking up the strand between the stitch just worked and the next stitch, placing it on the left needle and knitting into the back of it. Note that because increases are so concealed in this pattern, there is no need to make right- and left-leaning increases.

**Next Round.** Work (K1, P1) to end of round, slipping markers when you come to them and continuing the (K1, P1) sequence between markers.

**Next Round.** Knit to marker, slip marker. Work Round 1 of thumb gusset to next marker, slip marker. Knit to end of round.

**Next Round.** Work (K1, P1) to marker, slip marker. Work Round 2 of thumb gusset to next marker, slip marker. (P1, K1) to end of round.

Continue in patterns as set, working successive rounds of thumb gusset between markers and alternate rounds of Thermal pattern on all other stitches until gusset Round 10 is complete, finishing the round in Thermal.

**Next Round.** Removing markers as you come to them, knit to marker, slip 13 gusset stitches to a length of waste yarn. Cast on 3 stitches to bridge gap. Knit to end of round.

**Next Round.** Work (K1, P1) to end of round (42 stitches). Thumb gusset is complete.

Continue in Thermal until work measures 2 inches (5 cm) from desired finished length, ending with a knit and purl round. Top shaping will add 2 inches to the length. Count rounds to make sure both mittens are the same length.

## Shape Top

Arrange stitches on needles: 21, 11, 10.

**Set-Up. Next Round.** K1, place marker, K18, place marker, K3, place marker, K18, place marker, K2. This establishes a column of 3 pattern stitches at each side for borders.

**Shaping Round 1.** K1, slip marker. SSK, (P1, K1) until 2 stitches before next marker, K2tog, slip marker. P1, K1, P1, slip marker. SSK, (K1, P1) until 2 stitches remain before next marker, K2tog, slip marker. K1, P1.

**Shaping Round 2.** Knit to end of round.

**Shaping Round 3.** K1, slip marker. SSK, (K1, P1) until 2 stitches remain before marker, K2tog, slip marker. P1, K1, P1, slip marker. SSK, (P1, K1) until 2 stitches remain before marker, K2tog, slip marker. K1, P1.

**Shaping Round 4.** Knit to end of round.
   Repeat Shaping Rounds 1–4 until 18 stitches remain, ending with a knit and purl round.

**Next Round.** Knit to end of round, removing markers when you come to them. Break yarn leaving a long tail. Graft top of mitten using Kitchener stitch or join with Three-Needle Bind Off.

## THUMB

Transfer 13 thumb gusset stitches to 2 double pointed needles, join yarn and knit them. Pick up and knit 3 stitches at the base of the thumb, taking care to pick them up above purl, knit, and purl stitches (16 stitches). Note beginning of round.

**Next Round.** (K1, P1) to end of round. This resumes Thermal pattern.

**Next Round.** Knit.

Continue in Thermal for 15 more rounds or until work reaches the middle of the thumbnail, ending with a knit and purl round.

**Thumb Decrease Round 1.** (K1, K2tog) to last stitch, K1 (11 stitches).

**Thumb Decrease Round 2.** K2tog to last stitch, K1 (6 stitches). Break yarn, thread through remaining stitches knitwise, tighten and secure.

## FINISHING

Do not block or press.

## BIG SPLASH TRIVIA

**Kitchener Stitch or Three-Needle Bind Off?**

It's a good idea to be skilled at both methods when finishing the tops of mittens. We usually use Kitchener stitch on solid colour mittens and the bind off on Fair Isle mittens. The bind off is a fussy technique but it makes a very neat finish for both types of mittens, so don't rule it out. It's a choice.

We do not recommend Kitchener stitch on Fair Isle mittens because it adds a single colour joining row at the top, whereas the bind off maintains the S&P pattern at the top. It's a question of finesse.

# LANDFALL
## Cabled Fingerless Mitts

**DEGREE OF DIFFICULTY * Smooth Sailing**

A playful quick knit for new knitters and lovers of simplicity! Stitch-by-stitch and row-by-row instructions ease your learning curve. Landfall mitts are simple rectangles, knit flat and then easily seamed leaving an opening for the thumb. There is no troublesome gusset or wrist shaping to worry about and you'll get a good cable workout at the same time. A change of yarn and needles easily produces two sizes. You'll be making them hand over fist! Personalize with buttons or beads if desired, remembering that these items can be a choking hazard, especially for young children. Consider filling the spaces with knitted bobbles (see Ripple Wristers) or simple embroidery if preferred. Wear them alone or over gloves.

## SIZE

**Medium.** Length: 8.5 inches (21.5 cm), or as desired. Width: 5 inches (12.5 cm), unstretched and unseamed.

**Small.** Length: 7.5 inches (19 cm), or as desired. Width: 6 inches (15 cm), unstretched and unseamed.

## YOU NEED

**Medium.** 100 metres medium worsted weight yarn (Group 4). Samples were knit with Briggs and Little Heritage 100% wool yarn, and Briggs and Little Softspun Hand Painted (Group 4). Two 5.00 mm needles, markers, cable needle.

**Small.** 100 metres light worsted weight yarn (Group 3). Samples were knit with Briggs and Little Regal 100% wool yarn. Two 4.00 mm needles, markers, cable needle.

## GAUGE

Gauge is flexible in this pattern.

Instructions for left and right hands are identical unless otherwise noted.

## CAST ON

Cast on 36 stitches.

**Row 1.** Right side. P1, (K2, P2) to last 3 stitches, K2, P1.

**Row 2.** K1, (P2, K2) to last 3 stitches, P2, K1.
    Repeat these 2 rows once more.

**Set-Up. Row 1. Right Side. Right Hand.** P1, rib 19 stitches as established, place marker. P2, slip 3 stitches to cable needle and hold in back, K2, knit 3 stitches from cable needle, P2, place marker. Rib as established to end of row. **Left Hand.** P1, rib 6 stitches as established, place marker. P2, slip 3 stitches to cable needle and hold in back, K2, knit 3 stitches from cable needle, P2, place marker. Rib as established to end of row.

**Row 2. Wrong Side.** Rib as established to marker, slip marker. K2, P5, K2, slip marker. Beginning with P1, rib as established to end of row.

**Row 3.** Rib to marker, slip marker. P1, slip 1 stitch to cable needle and hold in back, K2, knit 1 stitch from cable needle, K1, slip 2 stitches from cable needle and hold in front, K1, knit 2 stitches from cable needle, P1, slip marker. Beginning with P1, rib to end of row.

**Row 4.** Rib to marker, slip marker. K1, P7, K1, slip marker. Rib to end of row.

**Row 5.** Rib to marker, slip marker. P1, K7, P1, slip marker. Rib to end of row.

**Row 6.** Rib to marker, slip marker. K1, P7, K1, slip marker. Rib to end of row.

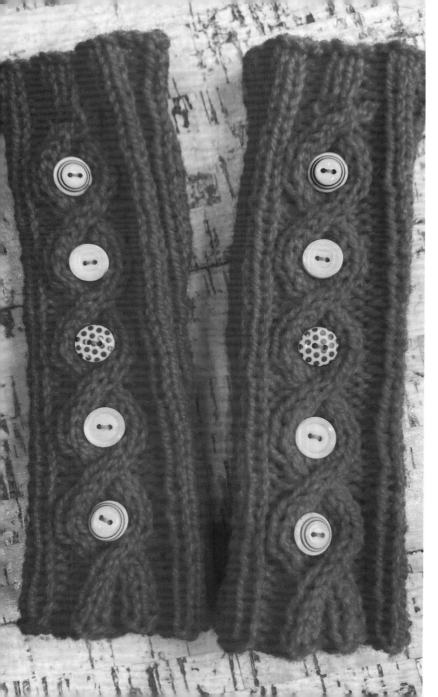

**Row 7.** Rib to marker, slip marker. P1, slip 2 stitches to cable needle and hold in front, P1, knit 2 stitches from cable needle, K1, slip 1 stitch to cable needle and hold in back, K2, P1 stitch from cable needle, P1, slip marker. Rib to end of row.

**Row 8.** Rib to marker, slip marker. K2, P5, K2, slip marker. Rib to end of row.

Repeat Rows 1–8 four times more, or to desired length, ending with Row 8.

Repeat Row 1 once.

**Decrease Row.** With wrong side facing, rib to marker, remove marker. K2, P2tog, P3tog, K2tog, remove marker. Rib to end of row.

Work 3 rows more in ribbing. Cast off in ribbing.

### FINISHING

Do not press or block. Attach buttons or beads if desired. With right side facing, sew selvages together, leaving a 2-inch (5 cm) opening for thumb beginning 1 inch (2.5 cm) below the top. If wearing Landfall mitts over gloves, a larger opening may be needed.

© Shirley A. Scott 2024

# HOLD FAST
## Wristers with a Message

**DEGREE OF DIFFICULTY ** Choppy**

In the days of sail, every mariner knew what the exhortation to hold fast meant. Lives depended on it. Sometimes the hardy sailors who went aloft in every sort of weather had the words tattooed on their knuckles. The expression may have originated in marine biology, but in the coronavirus pandemic "Hold Fast!" was the watchword of the province of Newfoundland and Labrador.

Note that in our design the words are readable to the wearer. If you want to send a message to the world instead, change both the position of the letters and the hands they are on.

## SIZE

Because of the number of stitches required, these wristers are often slightly large for most women and slightly small for most men. Varying stitch numbers is impractical, so knitters must change gauge for a custom fit. Be prepared to experiment. We have developed a range of sizes.

**Large.** At a gauge of 24 stitches = 4 inches, the circumference is 9 inches (22.5 cm). Length from beginning of Diamond pattern to cast off: 4.5 inches (11.5 cm). Samples were knit using Briggs and Little Heritage 100% wool (Group 4) and 4.00 mm needles.

**Medium.** At a gauge of 28 stitches = 4 inches, the circumference is 8 inches (20 cm). Length from beginning of Diamond pattern to cast off: 4.5 inches (11.5 cm). Samples were knit with Briggs and Little Regal 100% wool (Group 3) and 4.00 mm needles.

**Small.** At a gauge of 30 stitches = 4 inches, the circumference is 7 inches (18 cm). Length from beginning of Diamond pattern to cast off: 4.25 inches (11.0 cm). Samples were knit with Briggs and Little Sport 100% wool (Group 2) and 3.00 mm needles.

## YOU NEED

Two shades of yarn to produce desired size: 50 metres of Dark (D), small amount of Light (L). Knit the Hold Fast section in different colours if desired.

One set of 4.00 mm double pointed needles. Ring markers.

## DIAMOND Chart

Chart rows (bottom to top): 1, 2, 3, 4, 5, 6, 7, 8, 9, 10, 11, 12, 13, 14

## FAST Right Hand

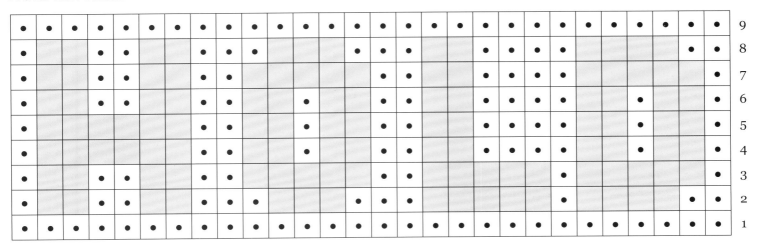

## HOLD Left Hand

## THUMB GUSSET Chart

Use Gusset A in Thumb Gussets in Words if preferred

Rows numbered right side: 18, 17, 16, 15, 14, 13, 12, 11, 10, 9, 8, 7, 6, 5, 4, 3, 2, 1

## CHART SYMBOLS

• K1D

➡ Make 1 Right with D

⇨ Make 1 Right with L

Empty square and shaded square = K1L

⬅ Make 1 Left with D

⇦ Make 1 Left with L

## Why Right- and Left-Leaning Increases in the Thumb Gusset?

In the old days this was seldom done, possibly because the technique was not known. In vintage mittens, any familiar type of increase was used. Most knitters used the "make 1 by pulling up a loop" method and, in their view, their mittens turned out just fine.

Technical standards have changed and this method is no longer favoured. In *Big Splash* patterns, increases in the thumb gusset must always be a specific colour and lean in a specific direction. If increasing by simply pulling up a loop, the required colour may not be in the right place when you need it. Knitters get around this by pulling up a float in the required colour, instead of correctly pulling up the bar that passes between stitches. This can leave a hole.

The "backward loop" (half-hitch) increase is a better choice. It's easy to control the colour and make it lean left or right as desired. Internet instructions are abundant.

O the ocean waves do roll,
And the stormy winds do blow,
And we poor sailors are skipping at the top,
While the landlubbers lie down below.

*Sea shanty*

## SALT AND PEPPER PATTERN (S&P)

**Round 1.** (K1D, K1L).

**Round 2.** (K1L, K1D).

Work charts from right to left, bottom to top.

For best results, carry D on the left (ahead) and L on the right.

On solid colour rounds, remember to carry the unused colour at the back, weaving it in loosely from time to time.

Note that on some thumb gusset rounds there will be 2 or more adjacent stitches of the same colour. This is corrected on the following round.

Instructions are for both hands and all sizes unless otherwise indicated.

## CAST ON

With D, cast on 42 stitches. Divide evenly on 3 needles and join in a circle, being careful not to twist. Work 30 rounds of (K2, P1) ribbing in a striped pattern of your choice.

**Next Round.** Knit, increasing 13 stitches evenly spaced (55 stitches). Arrange stitches on needles: 28, 14, 13.

**Set-Up. Round 1. Right Hand.** Join L and work Diamond Round 1 twice for the front of the hand (28 stitches). **Palm.** K1D, K1L, place marker. Make 1 right-leaning stitch with D,

In marine life, a holdfast is a rootlike structure that anchors aquatic organisms such as seaweed, algae, and sponges to a substrate. It is sometimes torn from the sea floor in storms.

K1D. Make 1 left-leaning stitch with D, place marker (K1L, K1D) to end of round.

**Set-Up. Round 1. Left Hand.** Join L and work Diamond Round 1 twice for the front of the hand (28 stitches). **Palm.** (K1D, K1L), repeat until 3 stitches remain in round, place marker. Make 1 right-leaning stitch with D, K1D. Make 1 left-leaning stitch with D, place marker. K1L, K1D.

This sets up 28 Diamond stitches on the front, S&P on the palm, with Round 1 of the thumb gusset between markers. Use Gusset A in Thumb Gussets in Words instead of chart if desired.

**Set-Up. Round 2. Both Hands.** Work Diamond Round 2 on 28 front stitches. Work S&P on palm to marker, slip marker. Work Round 2 of thumb gusset from chart or words to next marker, slip marker. Work S&P to end of round.

Continue in pattern as set until 14 rounds of Diamond and thumb gusset are complete, finishing the round in S&P.

Beginning with Diamond Round 1 and thumb gusset Round 15, continue in successive rounds of each pattern, ending with Diamond Round 4 and thumb gusset Round 18. Finish the round in S&P.

**Next Round. Front.** Work Diamond Round 5 twice. **Palm.** S&P to marker, remove marker. Place gusset stitches on a length of waste yarn, remove marker. Cast on 1 stitch with D to bridge the gap. Finish the round in S&P. Thumb gusset is complete.

**Next Round. Front.** Work Diamond Round 6 twice. **Palm.** S&P to end of round.

Continue with Diamond on front and S&P on palm until Diamond Round 7 is complete, finishing the round in S&P. **Next Round. Front. Right Hand.** Work Fast Round 1 once. **Left Hand.** Work Hold Round 1 once. **Both Hands. Palm.** S&P to end of round.

Working Fast or Hold on the front and S&P on palm, continue until Round 9 is complete, finishing the round in S&P. Break L.

With D, knit 2 rounds.

### Top Trim

**Decrease Round.** With desired colour work, (K2, P1, K2, P2tog) until 6 stitches remain in round. (K2, P1) to end of round.

Work 2 rounds more of (K2, P1) rib. Cast off in ribbing.

### Thumb Trim

Return thumb gusset stitches to 2 double pointed needles. Join desired colour and knit these stitches. Cast on 2 stitches at the base of the thumb (21 stitches). Work 2 rounds (K2, P1) rib. Cast off in ribbing.

**FINISHING.** Darn ends securely. Press lightly, omitting ribbing.

© Shirley A. Scott 2024

# MAKING WAVES
## Wristers, Classic Mittens, and Trigger Mitts

**DEGREE OF DIFFICULTY** * * * **Gale Force**

Is there a shortage of waves where you live? Make a few! Making Waves is a slow, careful design that requires patience and focus. The result is a spectacular work of art and a geometric feast of colour. To make the knitting voyage easier, read, mark, and inwardly digest our handy tips before beginning.

**SIZE**

**Medium.** Circumference: 8 inches (20 cm). Length of Wrister from beginning of Wave pattern: 4.5 inches (11.5 cm). Length of Classic Mitten and Trigger Mitt from beginning of Wave pattern: 7 inches (17.5 cm), or as desired.

**Large.** Circumference: 9.5 inches (24 cm). Length of Wrister from beginning of Wave pattern: 5 inches (12.5 cm). Length of Classic Mitten and Trigger Mitt from beginning of Wave pattern: 7.5 inches (19 cm), or as desired.

**YOU NEED**

Two or more shades of light worsted weight yarn (Group 3),

125 metres of Dark (D) and 125 metres of Light (L). Oddments are sufficient for multicoloured mittens. Samples were knit with Briggs and Little Regal 100% wool.

**Medium.** One set of 4.00 mm double pointed needles.
**Large.** One set of 5.00 mm double pointed needles.

Two thinner double pointed needles for trigger mitt bind off only (optional). Ring markers.

## GAUGE
**Medium.** 24 stitches and 28 rows = 4 inches (10 cm).
**Large.** 18 stitches = 4 inches (10 cm).

## SALT AND PEPPER PATTERN (S&P)
**Round 1.** (K1D, K1L).
**Round 2.** (K1L, K1D).

## WAVE Chart

| | | | | | | |
|---|---|---|---|---|---|---|
| • | • | • | • | • | • | 6 |
| • |  |  |  | • | • | 5 |
|  |  |  |  |  | • | 4 |
|  |  |  |  |  |  | 3 |
|  | • | • | • |  |  | 2 |
| • | • | • | • | • |  | 1 |

## THUMB GUSSET Chart
Follow Gusset B in the Gussets in Words section if preferred

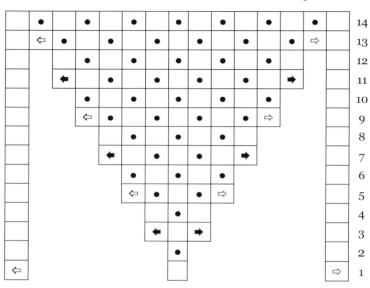

## CHART SYMBOLS

| | |
|---|---|
| • K1D | Empty square = K1L |
| ➡ Make 1 Right with D | ⬅ Make 1 Left with D |
| ⇦ Make 1 Left with L | ⇨ Make 1 Right with L |

Work charts from right to left, bottom to top. On solid colour Rounds 3 and 6 of Wave chart, carry the colour not in use at the back of the work, weaving it in at frequent intervals.

Instructions apply to both hands unless otherwise stated.

Always carry D on the left and L on the right, to prevent streaks in the colour work.

For multicoloured mitts, begin a new L colour on Round 1 or a new D colour on Round 4.

Note that some thumb gusset rounds will produce two or more adjacent stitches in the same colour.

## CAST ON

With D, cast on 36 stitches. Divide evenly on 3 needles and join in a circle, being careful not to twist. Work 25–30 rounds of (K2, P1) ribbing in a stripe sequence of your choice.

**Next Round.** With D, knit 1 round, increasing 13 stitches evenly spaced (49 stitches). Arrange stitches on needles as follows: 24, 12, 13.

**Set-Up. Round 1. Right Hand.** Join L and, keeping D ahead (on the left) throughout, work Round 1 of Wave chart four times for the front of the hand (24 stitches). **Palm.** K1L, K1D, place marker. Make 1 right-leaning stitch with L, K1L, make 1 left-leaning stitch with L, place marker. (K1D, K1L) to end of round.

**Set-Up. Round 1. Left Hand.** Join L and, keeping D ahead (on the left) throughout, work Round 1 of Wave chart four times, for the front (24 stitches). **Palm.** (K1L, K1D) until 3 stitches remain in round, place marker. Make 1 right-leaning stitch with L, K1L, make 1 left-leaning stitch with L, place marker, K1D, K1L.

**Both Hands.** The pattern is now established with 24 Wave stitches on the front, S&P stitches on the palm, and the thumb gusset between the markers.

**Set-Up. Round 2. Front.** Work Wave Round 2. **Palm.** Work in S&P to marker, slip marker. Work thumb gusset Round 2 to marker, slip marker. K1L, K1D. Follow Gusset B in Gussets in Words, if preferred.

Continue working successive Wave rounds on the front, S&P on the palm, and thumb gusset within the markers until thumb gusset Round 14 is complete. Finish the round in S&P. There are now 15 gusset stitches between markers.

**Next Round.** Work in patterns as established to marker, remove marker. Place 15 gusset stitches on a length of waste yarn as a holder, remove marker. Make 1 with L to bridge gap. Work in pattern to end of round. Thumb gusset is complete.

Continue working Wave on the front and S&P on the palm until 24 Wave rounds are complete. Finish the round in S&P.

Proceed to Classic Mittens or Trigger Mitts if desired.

## WRISTERS

**Top Trim. Next Round.** Knit 1 round with desired trim colour. (K2, P1, K2, P2tog) to end of round. Work 2 rounds of (K2, P1) rib. Cast off in ribbing.

**Thumb Trim.** Transfer thumb gusset stitches to 2 double pointed needles. Join colour of choice and knit these stitches. Pick up and knit 3 stitches at base of hand (18 stitches). Arrange work on 3 needles and work 2 rounds of (K2, P1) rib. Cast off in ribbing.

## CLASSIC MITTENS

**Next Round.** Joining the shade of L preferred to finish the hand, work Wave Round 1, completing the round in S&P.

**Next Round.** Beginning with K1D, work S&P to end of round. Continue in S&P for 10 rounds more, or until work reaches the tip of the little finger.

**Shape Top.** Use Two-Step Shaping, as follows. Note that some rounds will produce adjacent stitches of the same colour.

**Shaping Round 1. Front.** With Wave facing, K1 in correct colour. SSK with the next colour in the sequence. Resume S&P on the next stitch (having made 2 adjacent stitches of the same colour). Work in S&P until 3 stitches remain on front. K2tog in the same colour as the stitch just made. Work last stitch in correct colour of sequence. **Palm.** As front.

**Shaping Round 2. Front.** K1, SSK in next colour in the sequence. S&P until 3 stitches remain on front. K2tog in next colour in the sequence, K1.

**Palm.** As front. Correct colour sequence is restored. Repeat these 2 shaping rounds until 9 stitches remain. Break yarns, leaving a longer tail with one. Thread through remaining stitches knitwise and tighten.

Proceed to Thumb.

### TIPS

For multicoloured mitts, wind yarn into small balls of each shade. Only a few inches are needed for each pattern repeat and small balls are easier to control.

Count rows on the palm. It's easier.

## TRIGGER MITTS

**Next Round.** Join the preferred shade of L to finish the hand. This will also be the colour of the first stripe on the trigger finger. Work Wave Round 1 on front, S&P on palm.

**Reserve Trigger Finger Stitches. Right Hand.** With Wave facing and at the same edge as the thumb, place 6 stitches of the front on waste yarn. Place the corresponding 6 stitches of the palm on waste yarn. Beginning with K1D, work S&P on 18 remaining front stitches. Cast on 2 stitches in correct S&P sequence to bridge gap. Work S&P on palm to end of round.

**Reserve Trigger Finger Stitches. Left Hand.** Break yarns. With Wave facing and at the same edge as the thumb, place the first 6 stitches of the front on a holder. Place the corresponding 6 stitches of the palm on a holder. Rejoin yarns to first stitch of the front following the trigger finger. This is the new beginning of the round. Starting with K1D, work S&P on the front and palm. Cast on 2 stitches in S&P to bridge gap (39 stitches).

**Both Hands.** Arrange stitches: 19, 10, 10. Work in S&P for 12 rounds more or until mitten reaches the tip of the little finger.

**Shape Top.** Shape top using Three-Step Shaping as follows. Note that some rounds will produce adjacent stitches of the same colour.

**Shaping Round 1. Front.** With Wave facing, K1 in correct colour. SSK with the next colour in the sequence. Resume S&P on the next stitch (having made 2 adjacent stitches of the same colour). Work in pattern until 3 stitches remain on front. K2tog in the same colour as the stitch just made. Work last stitch in correct colour. **Palm.** As front.

**Shaping Round 2. Front.** K1, SSK in next colour in the sequence. S&P until 3 stitches remain on front. K2tog in next colour in the sequence, K1. **Palm.** As front. Correct colour sequence is restored.

**Shaping Round 3.** Work in S&P without decreasing. Repeat this three-round sequence twice more (15 stitches). Break yarns, leaving a 16-inch tail with one colour.

**Three-Needle Bind Off.** The hand is finished with a Three-Needle Bind Off on the wrong side of the work.

Place stitches of front on a length of waste yarn. Place stitches of palm on another length of yarn. Turn mitten inside out to work bind off on the wrong side using the long tail.

Return stitches on holders to 2 thinner double pointed needles for easier working. Hold these needles parallel to one another, the needle with the larger number of stitches at the front. With a third double pointed needle and the long tail, K1 from the front holding needle. Then knit 1 stitch from this needle together with 1 stitch of the opposite colour from the other needle: 2 stitches now on the working needle. Pass the first knit stitch over the second knit stitch on the working needle to cast it off. 1 stitch remains on working needle. Continue to knit together 1 stitch from front and rear holding needles and slipping the first stitch over second stitch on the working needle to cast off. Repeat until 1 stitch remains on working needle. Fasten off and darn ends. Turn work right side out.

### TRIGGER FINGER

Transfer trigger finger stitches to 2 double pointed needles.

**Right Trigger Finger.** With palm facing, rejoin yarns and work Wave Round 1 on 6 stitches of palm. Pick up and knit 6 stitches from the hand according to Wave Round 1. Arrange stitches: 6, 6, 6. **Next Round.** Work Wave Round 2 on 18 stitches.

**Left Trigger Finger.** With palm facing, work Wave Round 1 on 6 stitches of palm. Work Wave Round 2 on 6 stitches of front. This is the beginning of the round. Pick up and knit 6 stitches from the hand according to Wave Round 2. Work

## TIPS

Glorious multicoloured mittens create a lot of ends. Make friends with them. They provide warmth and reinforcement.

When picking up and knitting Wave stitches from the hand for the trigger finger, use a mixture of picked-up stitches and of make-1 stitches, in the correct colour order.

Wave Round 2 on the 6 palm stitches. Arrange stitches: 6, 6, 6.

**Both Hands.** This establishes 3 repeats of the Wave pattern on the trigger finger. Note that it is not necessary to carry the unused colour on Rounds 3 and 6 on the trigger finger.

    With Wave facing and beginning with Round 3, work successive Wave rounds until work reaches the tip of the index finger, ending with Wave Round 3 or 6. Break one colour and work finger decrease rounds with a single colour, as follows.

**Finger Decrease Round 1.** With D, (K1, K2tog) to end of round. **Finger Decrease Round 2.** K2tog to end of round. Break yarn. Thread through remaining stitches knitwise and secure.

## THUMB

Transfer 15 gusset stitches to 2 double pointed needles. Rejoin yarns and work these stitches in S&P.

    With a third needle, pick up and knit 4 stitches in S&P at the base of the thumb (19 stitches). Work 12 rounds more of S&P, or until work reaches the tip of the thumb.

**Thumb Decrease Round 1.** (K1 with correct colour in the S&P sequence, SSK with next colour in the sequence, K1 in

S&P), repeat to end of round working any leftover stitches in S&P. Adjacent stitches in the same colour will be eliminated in the next round.

**Thumb Decrease Round 2.** (K1 with correct S&P colour, SSK with next colour in the S&P sequence) to end of round working any leftover stitches in S&P. Break yarns. Thread through remaining stitches knitwise and secure.

## FINISHING

Darn ends securely. Press mitten lightly with steam or under a damp cloth. Do not press ribbing.

"I hope your finger is better now," Alice said very politely.

"Oh, much better!" cried the Queen, her voice rising into a squeal as she went on. "Much better! Be-etter, Be-e-ehh!" The last word ended in a long bleat, so like a sheep that Alice quite started.

She looked at the Queen, who seemed to have suddenly wrapped herself up in wool. Alice rubbed her eyes, and looked again. She could make nothing of it. She was in a little dark shop, and opposite her was an old Sheep, sitting in an armchair knitting.

"What is it you want to buy?" the Sheep said at last, looking up for a moment from her knitting.

"I don't quite know yet," Alice said, very gently.

"Are you a child or a teetotum?" the Sheep said, as she took up another pair of needles. She was now working with 14 pairs at once ...

Lewis Carroll, *Through the Looking Glass*

# TWO-WAY VAMPS
## One Design, Two Styles

**DEGREE OF DIFFICULTY** ** **Choppy**

Through the magic of simple arithmetic, two styles from the same instructions! Treetops and Making Waves stitch patterns are interchangeable in these Two-Way Vamps. Small repeating block patterns, a signature element of folk knitting, can be used in many different ways. This versatility emphasizes the kinship between popular traditional designs and helps guarantee their longevity.

Vamps are the slipper socks of Newfoundland. Originally designed to be worn as one layer in a system of footwear that worked both indoors and out, they are more likely to be displayed in the home in these energy-conscious days. The ankle and heel are roomy enough to make slipping on and off easy. For a bit of fun, make Two-Way Vamps as playful singles—it's one way of avoiding the Second Sock Scourge—or as lovable pairs.

Please note that vamps can be a slipping hazard.

## SIZE

**Medium.** Circumference of ribbed top: 9 inches (23 cm) unstretched. Length of ribbed top from cast on to heel flap: 3 inches (7.5 cm) or as desired. Circumference of foot: 8.5 inches (21.5 cm). Length of foot from back of heel to tip of toe: 9.5 inches (24 cm), or as desired.

**Large.** Circumference of ribbed top: 9 inches (23 cm) unstretched. Length of ribbed top from cast on to heel flap: 3 inches (7.5 cm), or as desired. Circumference of foot: 9.5 inches (24 cm). Length of foot from back of heel to tip of toe: 10.5 inches (26.5 cm), or as desired.

## YOU NEED

**Medium.** Main Colour (MC): 150 metres light worsted weight yarn (Group 3). Contrast Colours (CC): oddments of light worsted weight yarn (Group 3). Samples were knit with Briggs and Little Regal 100% wool.

One set of 4.00 mm double pointed needles.

**Large.** Main Colour (MC): 200 metres medium worsted weight yarn (Group 4). Contrast Colours (CC): oddments of medium worsted weight yarn (Group 4). Samples were knit with Briggs and Little Tuffy 100% wool.

One set of 5.00 mm double pointed needles.

## GAUGE

**Medium.** 24 stitches = 4 inches (10 cm).

**Large.** 22 stitches = 4 inches (10 cm).

## TREETOPS Chart

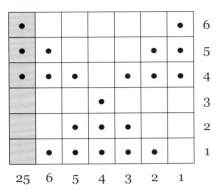

## MAKING WAVES Chart

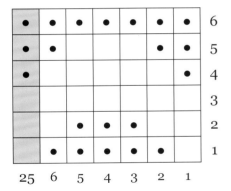

## CHART SYMBOLS

• K1 with Main Colour (MC)

Empty square = K1 with Contrast Colour (CC)

## SALT AND PEPPER PATTERN (S&P)

**Round 1.** (K1MC, K1CC).

**Round 2.** (K1CC, K1MC).

Instructions apply to both designs, unless otherwise noted.

Cast on 51 stitches with MC. Join in a circle, being careful not to twist. Divide stitches on 3 needles. Work (K2, P1) rib in a striped pattern of your choice for 3 inches (7.5 cm), or desired length.

**Next Row.** Knit to end of round.

### Set-Up Heel Flap

Turn the work so that the wrong side is facing. With a single needle, purl 26 stitches, increasing 1 stitch in the middle of the row (27 stitches). These stitches are the heel flap.

Arrange the remaining 25 instep stitches on 2 needles for flexibility. They become the front of the vamp after the heel flap is finished and the heel turned.

### Heel Flap

Worked flat on 2 needles. To begin, turn so right side is facing.

**Row 1.** Right side. (K1, slip 1 purlwise), repeat to last stitch, K1.

**Row 2.** Wrong side. Purl.

Repeat these two rows 13 times more. Heel flap is complete.

## Turn Heel

**Row 1.** Right side. K18, SSK, K1. Turn so that the wrong side is facing for next row.

**Row 2.** P11, P2tog, P1. Turn.

**Row 3.** K12, SSK, K1. Turn.

**Row 4.** P13, P2tog, P1. Turn.

**Row 5.** K14, SSK, K1. Turn.

**Row 6.** P15, P2tog, P1. Turn.

**Row 7.** K16, SSK, K1. Turn.

**Row 8.** P17, P2tog, P1 (19 stitches). Turn.

## Set-Up Instep

Return instep stitches to 1 double pointed needle. Divide the heel stitches on 2 needles for flexibility.

Always carry MC on the left (ahead) and the CC on the right. Introduce a new colour on pattern round 4 or 1, if de-sired. **Making Waves Only.** Carry the colour not in use on single-colour rounds, weaving it in at frequent intervals. This maintains a uniform texture.

**Next Round.** With right side facing, knit 19 heel stitches. Pick up and knit 14 stitches along adjacent edge of heel flap.

Rejoin CC and work stitches 1–6 of Round 1 of Treetops/Waves four times. Work stitch 25 (shaded). Break CC.

With MC, pick up and knit 14 stitches from heel flap.

Knit 19 heel stitches. Knit 14 stitches from heel flap (25 instep, 47 sole).

**Next Round. Instep.** Rejoin CC. This is the new beginning of the round. Work 25 stitches of Treetops/Waves Round 2. **Sole.** K1 with MC, SSK with CC. (K1MC, K1CC) until 3 stitches remain in round. K2tog with CC, K1 with MC (25 instep, 45 sole).

**Next Round. Instep.** Work Treetops/Waves Round 3. **Sole.** Work in S&P.

## Shape Instep

Note that some shaping rounds produce adjacent stitches of the same colour on the sole. These are eliminated on the following round.

**Shaping Round 1. Instep.** Work next round of Treetops/

My feet are usually numb with the cold when I work about the kitchen, and Morrill is long-suffering as a bedfellow.

One Christmas my brother Doug's wife sent me a hot water bottle and a few days later a blow torch arrived from Doug for Morrill. He had wanted one for ages to use on odd soldering jobs. But as he held it up and beamed with pleasure, this is what I heard.

"Gee! Doug certainly means me to have comfort this winter. Nights that the hot water bottle won't do the trick, I can apply the blow torch."

Evelyn Richardson,
*We Keep a Light*

Waves. **Sole.** K1 in S&P, SSK with next colour in sequence. Work in S&P until 3 stitches remain in round. K2tog with same colour as the stitch just made. K1 in S&P.

**Shaping Round 2. Instep.** Work next round of Treetops/Waves. **Sole.** K1 in S&P, SSK with next colour in sequence. Work S&P until 3 stitches remain in round. K2tog with next colour in sequence. K1 in S&P.

**Shaping Round 3. Instep.** Work Treetops/Waves on instep. **Sole.** Work S&P to end of round without decreasing.

Repeat these 3 shaping rounds until there are 50 stitches on needles (25 instep, 25 sole).

Note that toe shaping will add 2 inches (5 cm) to length.

**Next Round.** Work next round of Treetops/Waves on instep, S&P on sole.

Repeat this round until a total of 42 rounds of Treetops/Waves have been completed on the instep, or until work measures 2 inches (5 cm) from final length, ending with Treetops/Waves Round 3 or 6. Finish the round in S&P. Break yarns.

### Toe
Join toe colour.

**Shaping Round 1.** Knit.

**Shaping Round 2. Instep.** K1, SSK, knit until 3 stitches remain in instep, K2tog, K1. **Sole.** K1, SSK, knit until 3 stitches remain before end of round, K2tog, K1.

Repeat these 2 rounds until 26 stitches remain in round, ending with a knit round.

Repeat Shaping Round 2 only until 14 stitches remain. Knit 1 round.

Break yarn, leaving a long tail. Graft toe using the tail. See How to Graft in Kitchener Stitch.

### FINISHING
Press well with steam or under a damp cloth.

### Heel and Toe: Stockinette or Salt and Pepper?

To make Two-Way Vamps friendly to less-experienced knitters, the heel flap and heel turning are worked in a single colour. S&P is used only on the instep shaping and sole. In more complex vamp designs, the heel flap, heel, instep shaping, sole, and toe can all be in S&P, a challenge for experienced knitters.

The virtue of S&P patterns is their warmth and durability. Heels turned this way are sometimes known as "double heels." They are cushioned and long lasting but tricky to repair.

A stockinette heel in a single colour is thinner and a little less durable, but easier to knit and much easier to repair.

### Heel Flap: Stockinette, Salt and Pepper, or Slipped Stitch?

You will find Newfoundland vamps with each of these heel flap treatments. What's the difference between them?

A plain stockinette heel flap is the easiest to do by far. Thin and fragile, they develop holes quickly. But they are very easy to darn.

A S&P heel flap is thick and hard wearing, but the most difficult to make and to darn. It may also be the most beautiful.

A slipped stitch heel flap is our favourite. It's fun to make and is strong and sturdy but rather difficult to darn neatly. Note that if the heel flap has an even number of stitches, the right-side rows begin with slip 1, knit 1. If the number of stitches on the heel flap is odd, the right-side rows begin with knit 1, slip 1.

# BIG HOLIDAY STOCKING
## to Hang by the Chimney with Care

**DEGREE OF DIFFICULTY** * * * **Gale Force**

There were no special Christmas stockings when we were young children. We simply borrowed something big from Dad. This fine design is a sampler of the old familiar patterns used in our winter clothes. They are united by sturdy S&P sections, the bedrock of our traditional knitting. The Big Holiday Stocking captures the spirit of Christmas long ago.

Our stocking is a fine fat fellow. It's large enough to hold some sporting equipment, a few walnuts, some fudge, peppermint nobs, ribbon candy, chicken bones, barley toys, and possibly a musical instrument or two. Harmonicas may not be appreciated! The toe is generous enough for a delicious fresh orange, an exotic holiday treat in bygone days. There's lots of challenging knitting here to keep you on your toes.

See our suggestions for personalizing a stocking and tips for hanging before beginning.

## SIZE

**One Size.** Circumference: 15 inches (38 cm). Leg from cast on to heel flap: 12 inches (30.5 cm). Foot from back of heel to toe: 13 inches (33 cm).

## YOU NEED

Dye lot is not critical in this project. Oddments of light worsted weight yarn (Group 3) in seasonal colours of Red, Green, and White, or colours of your choice. A larger amount of White is needed because it is used throughout. Sample was knit with Briggs and Little Regal 100% wool.

One 4.00 mm circular needle, 40 centimetres long. A 60-centimetre-long needle may be preferred.

One set of 4.00 mm double pointed needles for heel flap, heel turning, and toe.

Ring markers.

## GAUGE

22 stitches = 4 inches (10 cm). Gauge is not critical in this project.

## CHARTS

● Red, Green, or Dark colour of choice.
Empty square = White or Light colour of choice.
Work all charts from right to left, bottom to top.

**Charts A, B, and C Only.** The centre section of the chart is repeated. The other two sections form an S&P border that facilitates jog-free syncing of the rounds. It lies at the back of the leg. Spaces between sections of the chart are for convenience only; they do not represent missing stitches. They separate the border from the repeating section. On the first round, you will insert a marker in these places to divide the sections.

## CAST ON

**Step 1.** With Red, cast on 84 stitches. Join in a circle, being careful not to twist. Mark the beginning of a round with a distinctive marker. Work 20 rounds or desired length in (K2, P1) ribbing, in a striped pattern of your choice. Knit 1 round with Red, increasing 5 stitches evenly spaced (89 stitches). Break Red.

## Step 2. Chart A

**Round 1.** Using Green and White, or colours of choice, work as follows. Knit first 3 stitches in S&P. Place marker. Repeat the 14 stitches in the centre of chart six times. Place marker. Work last 2 stitches in S&P.

**Step 3.** Work Rounds 2–18 of Chart A in this way, removing markers on last round. Break Green.

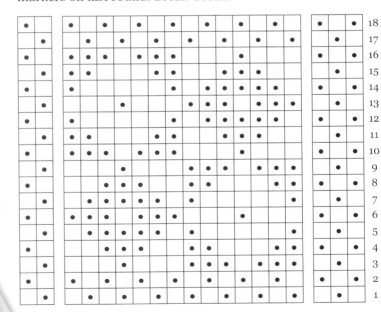

## Step 4. Chart B

Read suggestions about personalizing this section before beginning. This is the best place to do it if desired.

**Round 1.** Join Red. Work first 3 stitches of Round 1 once. Place marker. Work centre section of chart until 2 stitches remain in round. Place marker. Work last 2 stitches of the round once. Continue working Rounds 2–16 in this way, removing markers on last round. Break Red.

## TIPS for Hanging

Decide in advance how the stocking will hang, whether front forward or side forward.

Because it will become very heavy when filled, creating a loop on the cast-on edge for hanging is not practical. It will never be strong enough.

A buttonhole introduced at a suitable spot in the ribbing is a great idea. Another is to force a hole in the ribbing about 1.5 inches (4 cm) below the cast on. This gives better support and will not damage the stocking. Force the hole by simply hanging the stocking on a nail or hook.

## TIPS for Personalizing

Personalizing a stocking requires preparation. The most challenging way is to substitute a chart of your own for the stitches in the centre of Chart B. You have a total of 84 stitches and 16 rows to work with.

If you choose this method, create your own initials, or use one of the many knitting alphabets available on-line. Remember to leave space between each initial and each repeat on the chart. Very important: because this stocking is knit top down, it is essential to knit the chart that you create **upside down** for it to appear correct on the finished work. Leave a border of S&P stitches and rows surrounding your design to make it easier to knit. Make sure they sync with other rounds of S&P in the design.

Easier ways include substituting personalized favourite colours for one of the charts in the leg. Or substitute stripes for one of the charts, giving each stocking a distinctive stripe sequence.

You may also prefer to work Chart B in a single background colour, adding contrasting initials or symbols afterwards by embroidery, cross stitch, duplicate stitch, or needle felting. Plan the spacing carefully.

## Step 5. Chart C

**Round 1.** Join Green. Work stitches 1–3 of Round 1 once. Place marker. Work the 14-stitch repeating section six times. Place marker. Work remaining 2 stitches once.

Work Rounds 2–15 of Chart C in this manner.

Work Rounds 2–8 once.

Work Round 17, removing markers when you come to them.

## Step 6. Heel Flap

**Next Round.** Work 23 stitches in S&P. Break White. Turn the work so that the wrong side is facing.

With Green, purl 45 stitches for the heel flap and place them on 1 double pointed needle. Turn so that the right side is facing.

Arrange the remaining 44 stitches on 2 double pointed needles for flexibility, and leave them there until the heel is turned. The heel flap is now worked back and forth on 45 stitches with double pointed needles as follows. If making a striped pattern, join new colours as desired on a wrong side row.

**Heel Flap Row 1.** Right side. With another double pointed needle (K1, slip 1 purlwise) to last stitch. K1. Turn.

**Heel Flap Row 2.** Purl. Turn.
Repeat these 2 rows 15 times more, ending with a wrong-side row.

## Step 7. Turn Heel

With Green or the colour of your choice, knit 1 row, purl 1 row.

**Heel Row 1.** K30, SSK, K1. Turn.

**Heel Row 2.** P17, P2tog, P1. Turn.

**Heel Row 3.** K18, SSK, K1. Turn.

**Heel Row 4.** P19, P2tog, P1. Turn.

**Heel Row 5.** K20, SSK, K1. Turn.

**Heel Row 6.** P21, P2tog, P1. Turn.

**Heel Row 7.** K22, SSK, K1. Turn.

**Heel Row 8.** P23, P2tog, P1. Turn.

**Heel Row 9.** K24, SSK, K1, Turn.

**Heel Row 10.** P25, P2tog, P1. Turn.

**Heel Row 11.** K26, SSK, K1. Turn.

**Heel Row 12.** P27, P2tog, P1. Turn.

**Heel Row 13.** K28, SSK, K1. Turn.

**Heel Row 14.** P29, P2tog, P1. Turn (31 stitches).

Return stitches on front of stocking to 1 double pointed needle. Arrange the heel stitches conveniently on 2 double pointed needles.

### Step 8. Set-Up Instep

With another double pointed needle, knit 31 heel stitches. Pick up and knit 17 stitches along the adjacent edge of the heel flap. Join White and work 44 stitches of front in S&P. Break White. With Green, pick up and knit 17 stitches on the remaining side of the heel flap.

Knit 31 sole stitches and 17 picked-up stitches.

**Next Round.** Transfer stitches back to the circular needle and resume knitting in the round. Place a distinctive marker here to indicate the new beginning of the round. Join White again and work 1 round in S&P, adding a marker to separate front and sole.

### Step 9. Shape Instep

Note that some shaping rounds will produce adjacent stitches of the same colour. This is corrected on the following round.

**Instep Round 1.** Work 44 front stitches in S&P. **Sole.** Knit 1 in correct colour of S&P. SSK with next colour in the S&P sequence. Knit 1 with correct S&P colour. Continue in S&P until 3 stitches remain on sole. K2tog in same colour as the stitch just made. K1 in S&P.

**Instep Round 2.** Work S&P on 44 stitches of the front. **Sole.** K1 in the correct S&P colour. SSK in the next colour in the S&P sequence. Work in S&P until 3 stitches remain in the round. K2tog in next colour in the S&P sequence. Work last stitch in S&P.

**Instep Round 3.** Work in S&P without decreasing.

Changing colours in a striped pattern, if desired, repeat these 3 instep rounds until 87 stitches in round (44 front, 43 sole), ending with Instep Round 2. Instep is complete.

### Step 10. Chart D

Rearrange stitches on needles: 45 front, 42 sole. There are no S&P borders on Charts D and E. Note that S&P rows of chart and sole will not sync on every round.

Join a new D colour of your choice.

**Next Round. Front.** Work Chart D Round 1 seven times (42 stitches). Work stitches 1–3 of Round 1 (shaded area) once (45 stitches). **Sole.** S&P.

Work Rounds 2–8 of Chart D in this manner, continuing to work the sole in S&P.

Work Rounds 1–8 once more in this manner.

Work 2 rounds S&P. Break Red.

Left chart (Rounds 1–8):

| | | | | | | Round |
|---|---|---|---|---|---|---|
| | • | | • | | • | 8 |
| • | • | • | | | | 7 |
| • | • | • | | | | 6 |
| | • | | • | | • | 5 |
| • | | • | | • | | 4 |
| | | | • | • | • | 3 |
| | | | • | • | • | 2 |
| • | | • | | • | | 1 |

Right chart (Chart E, Rounds 1–14):

| 6 | 5 | 4 | 3 | 2 | 1 | Round |
|---|---|---|---|---|---|---|
| | | | • | • | • | 14 |
| | | • | • | • | | 13 |
| | • | • | • | | | 12 |
| • | • | • | | | | 11 |
| | • | | • | | • | 10 |
| • | | • | | • | | 9 |
| | • | | • | | • | 8 |
| • | • | • | | | | 7 |
| | • | • | • | | | 6 |
| | | • | • | • | | 5 |
| | | | • | • | • | 4 |
| • | | • | | • | | 3 |
| | • | | • | | • | 2 |
| • | | • | | • | | 1 |

## Step 11. Chart E

**Next Round. Front.** Join Green. Work Chart E Round 1 seven times (42 stitches). Work stitches 1–3 of Round 1 (shaded area) once (45 stitches). **Sole.** S&P.

Work Rounds 2–14 of Chart E in this manner, continuing the sole in S&P.

Work 3 rounds of S&P. Break Green.

### Step 12. Toe

Arrange stitches on double pointed needles as follows: 44 front, 21 and 22 sole. Join Red.

Note that some decrease rounds will produce adjacent stitches of the same colour. This is corrected on the following round.

**Toe Round 1. Front.** K1 in S&P, SSK with next colour in S&P sequence. Resume S&P until 3 stitches remain on front, K2tog with same colour as the stitch just made, K1 in S&P. **Sole.** As front.

**Toe Round 2.** K1 in S&P, SSK with next colour in the sequence. Work in S&P until 3 stitches remain on front, K2tog in correct S&P colour, work 1 S&P. **Sole.** As front.

Repeat Toe Rounds 1–2 until 9 stitches remain in round. Break yarn, leaving a long tail. Thread through remaining loops and pull tight.

### FINISHING

Bonus! Because a hanging stocking will never be worn, feel free to knot the ends securely on the inside instead of weaving them in. Press with steam.

© Shirley A. Scott 2024

## Photo Credits

P. Barry, 29.

L. Chatzikirou, 94.

7 Fathoms, 104 (bottom right).

J. Laaning, 146 (bottom right).

S. Minty, 113.

J. Ritcey, 19.

A. Sajovik, 10, 11, 12, 35, 92, 99,
120, 122, 123, 127, 143,
front cover.

K. Scott, 142 (top right).

C. Sheu, 8, 12, 15, 19, 22,
27, 39, 131, 134, 140, 141,
back cover (right).

L. Stark, 85.

Adobe Stock photos, 30, 37, 45,
53, 67, 74, 81, 107.

All other photos in this book
were taken by Shirley A. Scott.

# WORDS OF APPRECIATION

It may take a village to raise a child but it certainly takes quite a lot of people to make a knitting book. A willing group of expert, sharp-eyed test knitters took time from their personal knitting projects to prevent a lot of silly mistakes from reaching your eyes. Thanks to them forever. Happily, test knitting for *Big Splash Knits* ended just as gardening season began, a time when testers tend to melt into the greenery. Special thanks to Milly Brown for her wonderful work, her encouragement, and technical assistance. The others are Linda Badcock, Carolynn Sheu, Evelyn Reid Harrington, Maria Price do Soulas, Brigid McWhirter, Mary Dawn Greenwood, Lisa Chatzikirou, and the excellent staff of the Briggs and Little Woolen Mill in New Brunswick. Special thanks to Mary Pat McDonald for her sharp-eyed assistance.

We are so lucky to meet people who immediately sense our mission in life. Some of them understand it better than we do ourselves. Special thanks to Julie Vogt, who knows the significance of knitting in our cultural life and promotes it at every opportunity. A girl after my own heart.

Talented photographers shared their skill, creating a book rich with inspiring and thoughtful images that celebrate our way of life. Thanks to Paddy Barry, 7 Fathoms Skin Care, Brigid McWhirter, Katherine L. Scott, Lisa Chatzikirou, Ricky Brophy, Carolynn Sheu, Joan Ritcey, Lynn Stark, and Sarah Minty. Handsome and courageous models braved some very iffy weather to lend their personal images to our work. Thanks to Andrew Griffiths and Daniel Pineda-Griffiths, Glenn Day, Marcia Porter, Janet Harron, Megan Robbins, Amelia Martin, Libby Moore, Geoff Duffett, and Kelly Mansell.

A book without a publisher does not do much good or get very far in this world. The staff of Boulder Books are hard workers, each wearing many hats. Thank you for making my work easy and friendly. You do the work of angels.

My writer's heart swells with gratitude for the waves of encouragement of loyal fans and supporters everywhere. This book was written for you. Please enjoy it for years to come.

SAS, 2024

# MEET THE AUTHOR

Shirley Anne Scott, sometimes known as Shirl the Purl, has adored knitting since she was a child working away on her first project, a yellow scarf that came to resemble an amusing map of Africa. After a brief intermission for puberty and the sowing of wild oats, she took up needles once again and has never put them down. "To live is to knit" is her motto.

Shirl's knitting life has been a rich one, full of opportunities for historical research, designing, teaching, public speaking, writing, and travelling. The knitting world has been kind to her but in recent years the wonderful experience of moving to Newfoundland and teaming up with Christine LeGrow to write the *Saltwater* knitting books became the icing on her cake.

*Big Splash Knits* is her sixth book.